SCHOLARS
& Other
Deep Thinkers

VGM Careers for You Series

SCHOLARS
& Other
Deep Thinkers

Blythe Camenson

VGM Career Books
NTC/Contemporary Publishing Group

Library of Congress Cataloging-in-Publication Data

Camenson, Blythe.
    Careers for scholars & other deep thinkers / Blythe Camenson.
        p. cm. — (VGM careers for you series)
     ISBN 0-658-00191-4 (cloth). — ISBN 0-658-00192-2 (pbk.)
      1. Vocational guidance—United States.   2. Learning and scholarship.
   I. Title. Careers for scholars and other deep thinkers. II. Title. III. Series.
   HF5382.5.U5 C25193   2000
   331.7′0235—dc21   00–38189
                                                           CIP

*To all my university professors, who
guided me and satisfied my curiosity*

Published by VGM Career Books
A division of NTC/Contemporary Publishing Group, Inc.
4255 West Touhy Avenue, Lincolnwood (Chicago), Illinois 60712-1975 U.S.A.
Printed in the United States of America
International Standard Book Number: 0-658-00191-4 (hardcover)
                                         0-658-00192-2 (paperback)
01 02 03 04 05 LB 19 18 17 16 15 14 13 12 11 10 9 8 7 6 5 4 3 2 1

Contents

Acknowledgments   vii

CHAPTER ONE
Studying the Options: An Overview   1

CHAPTER TWO
College and University Professors   7

CHAPTER THREE
Librarians and Archivists   19

CHAPTER FOUR
Freelance Researchers   37

CHAPTER FIVE
Social Scientists   47

CHAPTER SIX
Psychologists   71

CHAPTER SEVEN
Museum Curators   89

CHAPTER EIGHT
Botanical Specialists   105

CHAPTER NINE
Animal Behaviorists   125

APPENDIX
Professional Associations   135

About the Author   151

Acknowledgments

T he author would like to thank the following scholars and other deep thinkers for providing information about their careers.

Anne Brennan	Student Intern
Susan Broadwater-Chen	Information Specialist
Judy Burns	Lecturer
Marshall J. Cook	Professor
Rick Darke	Curator of Plants
John Fleckner	Chief Archivist
Dave Foresman	Student Programs Coordinator
Ann Gardner	Social Anthropologist
Carol Jones	Technical Services Librarian
Susan Kelley	Curatorial Associate
Kristin Kuckelman	Field Archaeologist
Charles McGovern	Curator
Valarie Neiman	Academic Researcher
Mary Lee Nitschke	Animal Behaviorist
Steve Oserman	Reference Librarian
Gerald D. Oster	Clinical Psychologist
Chris Strand	Outreach Horticulturist
Denise Stybr	School Psychologist
Carolyn Travers	Director of Research
Jill Winland-Brown	Associate Professor

CHAPTER ONE

Studying the Options

An Overview

T here are those who can't wait for their final year of school. Graduation comes, up fly the caps, down go the books, and the only noise heard is the sound of feet rushing through the door and out into the real world.

Then there are those—you, most likely, if you're reading this book—who prefer the red brick and ivy, the musty stacks in the back of the library, the quiet halls during class time, the noisy conversation in the cafeteria.

You have spent years working on your undergraduate degree, preparing yourself for not a foray into the real world but yet another stint of educational pursuit. The world of academia is your calling, and, whether your goal is to stay within those hallowed halls or move into a comparable setting, in *Careers for Scholars*, you will find a variety of choices to suit your degree and interests.

Do You Have What It Takes?

What is a scholar? The dictionary defines it as a learned or erudite person, an individual who is educated and well-read, an intellectual and a thinker. A scholar is also a student, pursuing knowledge for knowledge's sake—and to pass it on to others.

Scholars are often experts in a particular body of knowledge, U.S. history, for example, or the culture of the Kalahari Bushmen in the deserts of Africa. They can be sociologists, historians, anthropologists, archaeologists, psychologists, animal behaviorists, botanists, horticulturists, museum curators, librarians, archivists, teachers, or they can wear a score of other academic and professional designations.

Although their academic training may vary, they share many same skills and interests. Scholars are excellent researchers; they spend a great deal of their time perusing reference books, periodicals, abstracts, and the growing volume of information available on the Internet.

Scholars often make excellent teachers, as well. Through their research and academic studies, they have become immersed in particular disciplines and are able to pass on their knowledge to others, whether through classroom interaction, talks and presentations, the written word, or any combination thereof. But teaching, research, and writing are not the only ways in which scholars use their skills and talents to make a living. Though most are thrilled by the discoveries of research, others are collectors or catalogers by nature. Whatever particular interest you, as a scholar, hold, you will find almost as many settings in which to work as areas of study to pursue.

Settings for Scholars

Universities and colleges are the most obvious settings for scholars, and it is true that a wide range of research and teaching does go on within those ivy-covered walls. However, scholars also find employment in the following settings:

- archives
- libraries
- museums
- botanical gardens

- zoos
- laboratories
- hospitals
- archaeological sites

In addition, certain scholars—often anthropologists, sociologists, or archaeologists—conduct research in the field, in Africa, for example, or in Samoa, Papua New Guinea, and even within the shores of North America.

Throughout this book we will explore a variety of settings where you, as a job-hunting scholar, might find your niche.

Job Titles for Scholars

Frequently, many job titles are common to each particular setting, but the job description will vary depending on the institution. Curators, for example, are found in almost every kind of museum, from art and science to history museums, as well as in botanical gardens, even though the collections they deal with and their specific duties are very different.

In *Careers for Scholars*, we will examine the following job designations:

- university professor
- genealogist
- museum curator
- botanical garden curator
- archaeologist
- anthropologist

- archivist
- librarian
- researcher
- psychologist
- animal behaviorist

This list is far from comprehensive—the settings and job titles for scholars can stretch to include all the different "ologies." As you set out on your job search in your own specialized area of study, you will be able to add to the suggestions here and create your own tailor-made inventory.

Heaven-Sent Jobs for Scholars

Job-hunting scholars dream of finding positions where their skills and interests can be combined. Would any of these help-wanted ads send you racing to the post office to mail off your resume?

Researcher University department seeks experienced researcher for project helping dissertation students.

_____

Dig Site Assistant Position open for energetic student or recent graduate at major archaeological dig site in New Mexico. Duties include cleaning and recording discovered artifacts.

_____

Information Officer Historic site preservation board has opening for officer to disseminate information to the public. Good writing skills necessary. Bilingual, Spanish/English a plus.

_____

University Instructor   Four-year liberal arts college seeks to fill a tenure-track position in the anthropology department. Duties include classroom teaching and student advising. Research budget available.

Assistant Collections Manager   Prestigious New York museum seeks master's level or above historian to work in the collection department. Knowledge of eighteenth-century European art a plus.

Do You Have the Necessary Qualifications?

Required qualifications vary depending on the job. Although many employers prefer their applicants to have master's degrees or even doctorates, others are satisfied with bachelor's degrees. In some situations, the following qualifications are equally important: experience, extensive knowledge of a particular time period or region, the ability to communicate with diverse groups of people, good writing skills, and research skills.

Salaries

Salaries vary widely from position to position but are generally low, as are most pay scales for education-related fields. Factors such as the source of funding or the region of the country have more impact on salary levels than the complexity of the job or the level of the candidates' education and experience.

Some jobs pay only hourly wages; others follow the federal government's GS scale. Most jobs provide benefits such as health insurance. But all the professional scholars showcased in the pages to come stressed that financial rewards were not the main reason, or even a consideration, in pursuing their chosen professions. The low pay is far outweighed by the satisfaction of doing work they love.

The Job Hunt

Although many scholars can find employment in their own hometowns—in a local university or historic house museum, for example—in order to broaden your opportunities, chances are you'll have to relocate. If you have a spot in mind where you'd like to work, a phone call or an introductory letter sent with your resume is a good way to start. If you would like some more ideas on possible locations, there are several directories listed at the end of various chapters that can lead you to interesting destinations.

Many professional associations produce monthly or quarterly newsletters with job listings and upcoming internships and fellowships. Some key addresses have also been provided for you in the Appendix.

CHAPTER TWO

College and University Professors

College and university faculty teach and advise more than fourteen million full-time and part-time college students and perform a significant part of our nation's research. They also study and meet with colleagues to keep up with developments in their fields and consult with government, business, nonprofit, and community organizations.

Faculty generally are organized into departments or divisions, based on subject or field. They usually teach several different courses within their departments: algebra, calculus, and differential equations, for example. They may instruct undergraduate or graduate students, or both.

College and university faculty may give lectures to several hundred students in large halls, lead small seminars, and supervise students in laboratories. They also prepare lectures, exercises, and laboratory experiments, grade exams and papers, and advise and work with students individually.

In universities, they also counsel, advise, teach, and supervise graduate student research. They may use closed-circuit and cable television, computers, videotapes, and other teaching aids.

Faculty keep abreast of developments in their fields by reading current literature, talking with colleagues, and participating in professional conferences. Some also do their own research to expand knowledge in their fields. They experiment, collect and analyze data, and examine original documents, literature, and other source material. From this, they develop hypotheses, arrive at conclusions, and write about their findings in scholarly journals and books.

Most faculty members serve on academic or administrative committees that deal with the policies of their institutions, departmental matters, academic issues, curricula, budgets, equipment purchases, and hiring. Some work with student organizations. Department heads generally have heavier administrative responsibilities.

The amount of time spent on each of these activities varies by individual circumstances and the type of institution. Faculty members at universities generally spend a significant part of their time doing research; those in four-year colleges, somewhat less; and those in two-year colleges, relatively little. However, the teaching load usually is heavier in two-year colleges.

College faculty generally have flexible schedules. They must be present for classes, usually twelve to sixteen hours a week, and for faculty and committee meetings. Most establish regular office hours for student consultations, usually three to six hours per week. Otherwise, they are relatively free to decide when and where they will work and how much time to devote to course preparation, grading papers and exams, study, research, and other activities. They may work staggered hours and teach classes at night and on weekends, particularly those faculty members who teach older students who may have full-time jobs or family responsibilities on weekdays. They have even greater flexibility during the summer and school holidays, when they may teach or do research, travel, or pursue nonacademic interests.

Most colleges and universities have funds used to support faculty research or other professional development needs, including travel to conferences and research sites.

Part-time faculty generally spend little time on campus, since they usually don't have an office. In addition, they may teach at more than one college, requiring travel between their various places of employment.

Faculty members may experience a conflict between their responsibilities to teach students and the pressure to do research. This may be a particular problem for young faculty seeking advancement. Increasing emphasis on undergraduate teaching performance, particularly at small liberal arts colleges, in tenure decisions may alleviate some of this pressure, however.

Training

Most college and university faculty are in four academic ranks: professor, associate professor, assistant professor, and instructor. A small number are lecturers.

Most faculty members are hired as instructors or assistant professors. Four-year colleges and universities generally hire doctoral degree holders for full-time, tenure-track positions but may hire master's degree holders or doctoral candidates for certain disciplines, such as the arts, or for part-time and temporary jobs.

Doctoral programs usually take four to seven years of full-time study beyond the bachelor's degree. Candidates usually specialize in a subfield of a discipline, for example, organic chemistry, counseling psychology, or European history, but they also take courses covering the whole discipline. Programs include twenty or more increasingly specialized courses and seminars plus comprehensive examinations on all major areas of the field. They also include a dissertation, a report on original research to answer some significant question in the field.

Students in the natural sciences and engineering usually do laboratory work; in the humanities, they study original documents and other published material. The dissertation, done under the guidance of one or more faculty advisors, usually takes one or two years of full-time work.

In some fields, particularly the natural sciences, some students spend an additional two years on postdoctoral research and study before taking a faculty position.

A major step in the traditional academic career is attaining tenure. Newly hired faculty serve a certain period (usually seven years) under term contracts. Then, their records of teaching, research, and overall contributions to the institution are reviewed; tenure is granted if the review is favorable and positions are available. With tenure, a professor cannot be fired without just cause and due process. Those denied tenure usually must leave the institution. Tenure protects the faculty's academic freedom, the ability to teach and conduct research without fear of being fired for advocating unpopular ideas. It also gives both faculty and institutions the stability needed for effective research and teaching and provides financial stability for faculty members. About 60 percent of full-time faculty are tenured, and many others are in the probationary period.

Some faculty—based on teaching experience, research, publication, and service on campus committees and task forces—move into administrative and managerial positions, such as departmental chairperson, dean, and president. At four-year institutions, such advancement requires a doctoral degree.

Job Outlook

Employment of college and university faculty is expected to increase about as fast as the average for all occupations through the year 2005 as enrollments in higher education increase. Many additional openings will arise as faculty members retire. Faculty retirements should increase significantly through 2005 as a large number of faculty who entered the profession during the 1950s and 1960s reach retirement age at this time.

Enrollments increased in the early and mid-1980s despite a decline in the traditional college-age (eighteen to twenty-four) population. This resulted from a higher proportion of eighteen-to twenty-four-year-olds attending college, along with a growing number of part-time, female, and older students. Enrollments are expected to continue to grow through the year 2005, particularly as the traditional college-age population began increasing after the mid-1990s, when the leading edge of the baby-boom echo generation (children of the baby boomers) reached college age.

In the past two decades, keen competition for faculty jobs forced some applicants to accept part-time or short-term academic appointments that offered little hope of tenure; others sought nonacademic positions. This trend of hiring adjunct or part-time faculty should continue for some time due to the financial difficulties many universities and colleges are facing.

Many states have reduced funding for higher education. As a result, colleges increased the hiring of part-time faculty to save money on pay and benefits.

Job prospects will continue to be better in certain fields such as business, engineering, health science, computer science, physical sciences, and mathematics, largely because very attractive nonacademic jobs will be available for many potential faculty.

Employment of college faculty also is related to the nonacademic job market through an echo effect. Excellent job prospects in a field—for example, computer science from the late 1970s to the mid-1980s—cause more students to enroll, increasing faculty needs in that field. On the other hand, poor job prospects in a field, such as history in recent years, discourages students and reduces demand for faculty.

Salaries

Earnings vary according to faculty rank and type of institution and, in some cases, by field. Faculty in four-year institutions earn higher salaries, on the average, than those in two-year schools.

According to a 1994–95 survey by the American Association of University Professors, salaries for full-time faculty on nine-month contracts averaged $49,500. By rank, the average for professors was $63,500; associate professors, $47,000; assistant professors, $39,100; lecturers, $32,600; and instructors, $29,700. Those on eleven- or twelve-month contracts obviously earned more. In fields where there are high-paying nonacademic alternatives—notably medicine and law but also engineering and business, among others—earnings exceed these averages. In others—the fine arts, for example—they are lower.

Many faculty members have added earnings, both during the academic year and the summer, from consulting, teaching additional courses, research, writing for publication, or other employment.

Most college and university faculty enjoy some unique benefits, including access to campus facilities, tuition waivers for dependents, housing and travel allowances, and paid sabbatical leaves. Part-time faculty have fewer benefits than full-time faculty.

What It's Really Like

What better way to get a feel for a particular career path or job setting than to hear from a professional actively working in the field. The following three university teachers will give you an inside view of academia.

Jill Winland-Brown, Associate Professor, Florida Atlantic University

Jill Winland-Brown is a nurse *and* a doctor—a doctor of education. She teaches future nurses at Florida Atlantic University in Boca Raton, Florida. She has been an R.N. for twenty-five years and a university professor for fifteen years. She started her training in a three-year diploma program and earned her R.N. She worked for seven years and then went back to earn her bachelor's, then her master's, then, finally, her doctorate. She worked as a nurse throughout her studies.

"There are three components to my work: teaching, service, and research," Professor Winland-Brown explains. "I teach clinical and theory courses such as nursing ethics, leadership management, and technological skills (giving medications, starting IVs, and so forth) twelve hours a week. In addition, there's preparing lessons and grading papers.

"The service part of my job means giving something back to the community and to the university. I serve on a lot of boards and committees. I advise undergraduate and graduate students and help them with independent studies or with their theses or dissertations.

"When you're a professor, you're expected to do research, to further your own knowledge and that of others in important areas. Some of my research topics have involved problems for disabled nurses and summer camp nursing. You write papers to report what you've learned, and you submit these papers to professional journals for publication. I probably do a little of each—teaching, service, research—in any one day.

"What I love most about my work, though, is watching my students learn and mature and then go on to find rewarding careers. I like working with a wide range of students, whether they're freshmen or seniors or master's students or R.N.s coming back to earn their bachelor's degrees. Every day you could see one of each; it's almost like seeing them grow in the same day.

"I'm an advisor to many students, too. They're assigned to me when they first begin, and they stay with me all the way through. I like being able to follow them through their educations and to get to know them well.

"I also enjoy being near people who are working in a variety of disciplines. Most hospital nurses work only with other health care professionals. In a university setting, you come in contact with all different kinds of people.

"But we have to serve on a large number of committees. They take up a lot of time. And for university professors there's also the pressure of 'publish or perish.' You're expected to write articles and have them published in professional journals. You might spend a lot of time on two different papers; one gets published right away, the other you might have to submit several times, but they're both of equal value. It takes a lot of time."

Judy Burns, Adjunct Lecturer, University of California, Los Angeles

Judy Burns teaches screenwriting classes at UCLA Extension and in UCLA's M.F.A. program. She has had an extensive career in television including writing for shows such as "Star Trek," "Mission Impossible," "The Fugitive," "Toma," "Vegas," "T.J. Hooker," "Marcus Welby, M.D.," "Lucas Tanner," and "MacGyver." She also teaches screenwriting classes on America Online.

"This year I taught a class at University of California, Riverside, and Ithaca College in New York and at UCLA Extension and UCLA in the M.F.A. program," she recalls. "Next year I'm hoping my load will increase at UC Riverside, and the year after that it would be nice to be on a tenure track at the associate professor level. Nothing is definite yet.

"At UCLA Extension I teach Introduction to Screenwriting and Fixing Your Script, which is a rewrite class. I'll also be teaching 'Star Trek' and the Craft of Screenwriting, which is a specialty class I love to teach.

"I'm in the classroom six hours a week for the two classes. But then I also give office hours. I usually spend a few hours a week meeting with students. Then there's preparation and grading, so for a three-hour class I probably put in double hours a week for it. But of course I only get paid for the actual classroom hours.

"Concurrently I am teaching a graduate course in the School of Theater, Film, and Television at UCLA, and this class is a version of Fixing Your Script called Polishing Your Script.

"They called me over to teach this class because of my work in the Extension program. It's the first time they've ever had a rewrite class in the history of the program.

"I like the constant contact with the kids. I find that writers who work in a little room sometimes become too introspective and don't maintain contact with humanity—which is what they need to write and talk about. The constant influx of new ideas is great—you absorb all of that.

"The only downside is that it takes time away from my own writing, that I have to set aside specific time to do my own work. But that's the only downside. I love the kids and they love me."

Judy Burns's Background

Judy Burns has a bachelor of arts degree in anthropology from the University of California at Irvine. Years later she went back for a master's at Cal State in San Bernadino in 1989. It was an interdisciplinary major in theater, English, and history. She also earned a doctorate in critical studies in theater at UCLA.

"I came up through Hollywood as a story editor and producer, which means I was taught how to be these things and was taught by very good people. So, basically, I was on the other side of the desk every day dealing with writers who came to sell stories to me. I was passing on what I understood, and I think probably in 1989 I suddenly said to myself—you know all this information, it's time to pass it on.

"But then I realized that in order to pass it on properly I would have to understand the roots of screenwriting. I had come into screenwriting through the back door. I became a screenwriter because basically I needed money. I was in school studying anthropology, and I needed money for a ticket to Africa. I wanted to go dig bones.

"And here I was suddenly selling, then on staff. I was a writer, but I'd never had any academic training for it. I was a transplanted anthropologist. It's not a bad background, that and psychology, but I'd never had Shakespeare courses or drama or read a Tennessee Williams play. But I had a knack for writing, and I had read all my life.

"All my credits are in television. I broke in on 'Star Trek.' The show I wrote won an Emmy for special effects; it's called 'The Tholian Web.'

"I don't want to disillusion young people, but I had managed to work consistently for twenty years and then decided to go back to school and teach what I know. I'd rather be poor and refreshed, constantly in contact with students. There comes a time when you have to give it back and fill up your own container. After twenty years I felt depleted. By going back to school, I had the time to read and then took teaching assistant positions and was suddenly in contact with young people, and my universe expanded beyond just television. What I found was that the more I read, the more I absorbed, and I then almost immediately began to teach these things. I learned to appreciate teaching as an art form."

Some Advice from Judy Burns

"In order to become an instructor, you have to have a good long history of working in a particular profession or you need to get a degree, at least a master's or preferably a doctorate. You have to be willing to invest the time to do that. A bachelor's degree won't get you very far."

Marshall J. Cook, Professor, University of Wisconsin, Madison

Marshall Cook is a full professor in the Department of Communication Programs within the Division of Continuing Studies at the University of Wisconsin, Madison. He is also a writer with hundreds of articles to his credit, a couple of dozen short stories, and numerous books, including *Writing for the Joy of It, Freeing Your Creativity, How to Write with the Skill of a Master and the Genius of a Child, Slow Down and Get More Done, Leads and Conclusions*, and *Hometown Wisconsin*.

Before moving to Wisconsin, Cook was also an instructor at Solano Community College in Suisun City, California, for eight years.

"My job is really wonderful, and it's really different from the traditional campus teacher," Cook explains. "The Division of Continuing Studies is a separate division within the university, and our primary mission is adult education. I do a lot of workshops and some consulting and some on-site training of newspaper people, corporate communicators, and a variety of other people. For example, I run media workshops for cops called Preparing To Be Interviewed by the Press and one on newsletters that I've done for sixteen years. Another workshop is on stress management, and it follows the title of my book, *Slow Down and Get More Done.*

"Basically, I offer anything we can sell to the public. We're an income-generating unit, unlike campus teaching, and we're responsible for paying our own way.

"I develop the workshops and help publicize them and teach them, too. I'll personally teach maybe sixty to seventy of these a year, along with guest speaking and speaking at conferences and helping at other conferences.

"I teach much more than the average professor in a university, but there's no research component to my job. My research is all practical, and my publications are all mass media because that's what I teach.

"It's diverse—one of those rare opportunities to combine writing with another career that feeds the writing rather than detracting from it. The writing helps me teach, and the teaching helps me write.

"It's very stimulating, but it can be enormously tiring. I do a lot of traveling, mostly within the state, bringing the workshops to where the people are. We have down times, around Christmas or in the summer, but we do have busy seasons, too, and when it's hot, it's hot. Sometimes I have to do three workshops in a week. I have to be careful not to overschedule myself."

Marshall Cook's Background

Marshall Cook has a B.A. in creative writing from Stanford and an M.A. in communications/print journalism, also from Stanford. "I went to law school for about four months, and I was teaching one class at the University of Santa Clara in California. I realized I didn't want to be a lawyer. I liked studying the law but not the actual different jobs lawyers do, so I bailed out of that.

"At about that time, one of the teachers at Santa Clara died, and I got his job; they hired me full-time. I worked there four years in the English department. It was like an old dream had been reborn. Ever since I was a kid the only two things I really wanted to do was to be a teacher and a writer. Now I've found something that lets me do both. I got the class at Santa Clara basically just to make a few bucks to put myself through law school, and I discovered I really liked it. I don't think I was really that good at it at first, but it really appealed to me.

"I came to the University of Wisconsin in 1979 as a member of the academic staff as a program coordinator. I'm probably the last person in the system who came in this way, but at that time you could move from the academic staff track to what they call a tenure track. So I moved into being an assistant professor, which is a professor without tenure. Then I put in my requisite five to six years, then applied for tenure at the associate professor level. Once you hit that rank, it's with tenure. Another three years after that I applied and then became a full professor."

Some Advice from Marshall Cook

"These days, to become a full professor on a tenure track you'd need to get your Ph.D., and it should be in a field you have some passion for. It's a wonderful thing if you get the chance to do it because you not only deal in ideas, but you get to share them and watch them grow as you interact with young minds that aren't nearly as trained as yours but are flexible and hungry for the knowledge you have."

CHAPTER THREE

Librarians and Archivists

*L*ibrarians and archivists are excellent at research, one of the primary activities in which scholars indulge. Librarians make information available to people. They manage staff, oversee the collection and cataloging of library materials, and develop and direct information programs for the public. They help users find information from printed and other materials.

Archivists handle collections that chart the course of daily life for individuals and businesses. Some archives contain materials created by a specific institution. Coca Cola, for example, set up an archives years ago to have a history of what the company business was and how it prospered. New companies set up archives to keep a documented record. Other institutions, such as universities or museums, create archives that relate to their special research interests.

Nobody knows the exact number, but it's estimated that there are close to five thousand archives in the United States. Each of the fifty states maintains a government archives as well as do most city and county governments. Archives will also be found in universities, historical societies, museums, libraries, and private businesses. On the national level, the National Archives in Washington, D.C., looks after the records of the federal government. The Library of Congress provides information services to the U.S. Congress and technical services to all the libraries across the country.

Although archives are similar to libraries, there are distinct differences between the two. Libraries typically house materials that are published and were created with the express purpose of broad dissemination.

Library work is divided into three basic functions:

- User services

- Technical services

- Administrative services

Librarians in user services—for example, reference and children's librarians—work directly with users to help them find the information they need. This may involve analyzing users' needs to determine what information is appropriate and searching for, acquiring, and providing the information to users.

Librarians in technical services, such as acquisitions librarians and catalogers, acquire and prepare materials for use and may not deal directly with the public.

Librarians in administrative services oversee the management of the library, supervising library employees, preparing budgets, and directing activities to see that all parts of the library function properly. Depending on the employer, librarians may perform a combination of user, technical, and administrative services.

In small libraries or information centers, librarians generally handle all aspects of the work. They read book reviews, publishers' announcements, and catalogs to keep up with current literature and other available resources, and they select and purchase materials from publishers, wholesalers, and distributors.

Librarians prepare new materials for use by classifying them by subject matter and describe books and other library materials in a way that users can easily find them. They supervise assistants who prepare cards, computer records, or other access tools that indicate the title, author, subject, publisher, date of publication, and location in the library.

In large libraries, librarians often specialize in a single area, such as acquisitions, cataloging, bibliography, reference, special collections, circulation, or administration.

Librarians also compile lists of books, periodicals, articles, and audiovisual materials on particular subjects, and they recommend materials to be acquired. They may collect and organize books, pamphlets, manuscripts, and other materials in a specific field, such as rare books, genealogy, or music.

In addition, they coordinate programs such as storytelling for children and book talks for adults; publicize services; provide reference help; supervise staff; prepare the budget; and oversee other administrative matters. Librarians may be classified according to the type of library in which they work:

- Public libraries

- School libraries or media centers

- Academic libraries

- Special libraries

They may work with specific groups, such as children, young adults, adults, or disadvantaged individuals. In school libraries or media centers, librarians help teachers develop curricula, acquire materials for classroom instruction, and sometimes team teach.

Librarians may also work in information centers or libraries maintained by government agencies, corporations, law firms, advertising agencies, museums, professional associations, medical centers, religious organizations, and research laboratories.

Librarians build and arrange the organization's information resources, usually limited to subjects of special interest to the organization. These special librarians can provide vital information services by preparing abstracts and indexes of current periodicals, organizing bibliographies, or analyzing background information on areas of particular interest. For instance, a librarian working for a corporation may provide the sales department with information on competitors or new developments affecting the field.

Many libraries are tied into remote databases through their computer terminals, and many also maintain their own computerized databases. The widespread use of automation in libraries makes database searching skills important to librarians. Librarians develop and index databases and help users develop searching skills to obtain the information they need.

Libraries may employ automated-systems librarians who plan and operate computer systems and information scientists who design information storage and retrieval systems and develop procedures for collecting, organizing, interpreting, and classifying information.

The increasing use of automated information systems enables some librarians to spend more time analyzing future information needs as well as managing administrative and budgeting responsibilities and to delegate more technical and user services to technicians.

Working conditions in user services are different from those in technical services. Assisting users in obtaining the information for their jobs or for recreational and other needs can be challenging and satisfying. When working with users under deadlines, the work may be busy, demanding, and stressful.

In technical services, selecting and ordering new materials can be stimulating and rewarding. However, librarians may sit at desks or at computer terminals all day. Extended work at video display terminals may cause eyestrain and headaches. Librarians may also have their performance monitored for errors or for quantity of tasks completed each hour or day.

Nearly one out of four librarians works part-time. Public and college librarians often work weekends and evenings. School librarians generally have the same workday schedule as classroom teachers and similar vacation schedules. Special librarians usually work normal business hours.

Librarians in fast-paced industries, such as advertising or legal services, may work more than forty hours a week under stressful conditions.

Archives typically hold materials that were created in the course of carrying out some sort of business or activity but that were never intended originally for public dissemination. For example, in an archives you might find letters from a Civil War soldier to his family. He wrote about his experiences and feelings and to let his loved ones know that he was still alive, surviving this or that battle. He never would have imagined that his correspondence would one day appear in an archives. This gives his letters credibility, an integrity as a historical source. The newspaper reporter covering the same battles is writing with a specific point of view for widespread publication, ultimately with the intention of selling newspapers.

The material found in an archives can be letters, personal papers, organizational records, and other documents. Archives created within the last hundred years or so could also contain visual records such as photographs and postcards, prints, drawings, and sketches.

Today, archives also collect recording tapes, phonograph records, movie films, videotapes, and computer-stored information. Because archives hold firsthand information, they are valuable to anyone with an interest in the people, places, and events of the past. This group includes genealogists, museum researchers, scholars and students, writers, and historians.

Training

Librarians

A master's degree in library science (M.L.S.) is necessary for librarian positions in most public, academic, and special libraries and in some school libraries. In the federal government, an M.L.S. or the equivalent in education and experience is needed. Many colleges and universities offer M.L.S. programs, but many employers prefer graduates of the approximately sixty schools accredited by the American Library Association. Most M.L.S. programs require a bachelor's degree; any liberal arts major is appropriate.

Some programs take one year to complete; others take two. A typical graduate program includes courses in the foundations of library and information science, including the history of books and printing, intellectual freedom and censorship, and the role of libraries and information in society. Other basic courses cover material selection and processing; the organization of information; reference tools and strategies; and user services. Course options include resources for children or young adults; classification, cataloging, indexing, and abstracting; library administration; and library automation.

The M.L.S. provides general, all-round preparation for library work, but some people specialize in a particular area such as archives, media, or library automation.

A Ph.D. in library and information science is advantageous for a college teaching or top administrative position, particularly in a college or university library or in a large library system.

In special libraries, a knowledge of the subject specialization or a master's, doctoral, or professional degree in the subject is highly desirable. Subject specializations include medicine, law, business, engineering, and the natural and social sciences. For example, a librarian working for a law firm may also be a licensed attorney, holding both library science and law degrees. In some jobs, knowledge of a foreign language is needed.

State certification requirements for public school librarians vary widely. Most states require that school librarians, often called library media specialists, be certified as teachers and have courses in library science. In some cases, an M.L.S., perhaps with a library media specialization, or a master's in education with a specialty in school library media or educational media is needed. Some states require certification of public librarians employed in municipal, county, or regional library systems.

Experienced librarians may advance to administrative positions, such as department head, library director, or chief information officer.

Archivists

The standard way to become an archivist is to have an undergraduate degree with a history background and a graduate degree at least at the master's level that would involve specific course work in archives. There are thirty to fifty educational programs (the Society of American Archivists publishes a directory) that are often available in graduate library schools.

Many archivists have a master of library science degree (M.L.S.) with a concentration in archives, but sometimes archives courses are also taught in history departments.

Archivists need analytical ability to understand the content of documents and the context in which they were created and to decipher deteriorated or poor quality printed matter, handwritten manuscripts, or photographs and films. Archivists also must be able to organize large amounts of information and write clear instructions for its retrieval and use.

Job Outlook

Librarians

Employment of librarians is expected to grow more slowly than the average for all occupations through the year 2005. The limited growth in employment of librarians since the 1980s is expected to continue. However, the number of job openings resulting from the need to replace librarians who leave the occupation is expected to increase by 2005, as many workers reach retirement age. Willingness to relocate will greatly enhance job prospects.

Budgetary constraints will likely contribute to the slow growth in employment of librarians in school, public, and college and university libraries. The increasing use of computerized information storage and retrieval systems may also dampen the demand for librarians. For example, computerized systems make cataloging easier, so this task can now be handled by other library staff.

In addition, many libraries are equipped for users to access library computers directly from their homes or offices. These systems allow users to bypass librarians and conduct research on their own. However, librarians will be needed to define users' needs and to help users develop database searching techniques.

Childrens' librarians will be the least affected by information technology since children need special assistance.

Opportunities will be best for librarians outside traditional settings. Nontraditional library settings include information brokers, private corporations, and consulting firms. Many companies are turning to librarians because of their excellent research and organizational skills and their knowledge of library automation systems.

Librarians can review the vast amount of information that is available and analyze, evaluate, and organize it according to a company's specific needs. Librarians working in these settings are often classified as systems analysts, database specialists, managers, and researchers.

Archivists

Employment of archivists is expected to increase about as fast as the average for all occupations through the year 2005. Although the rate of turnover among archivists is relatively low, the need to replace workers who leave the occupation or stop working will create some additional job openings.

While federal government archival jobs are not expected to grow, new archival jobs are expected in other areas, such as educational services and state and local government. Archival jobs also will become available as institutions put more emphasis on establishing archives and organizing records and information. Despite the anticipated increase in the employment of archivists, competition for jobs is expected to be keen. Graduates with highly specialized training, such as a master's degree in library science with a concentration in archives or records management, may have the best opportunities for jobs as archivists.

Salaries

Librarians

Salaries for librarians vary by the individual's qualifications and the type, size, and location of the library. Based on a survey by the American Library Association, the average salary of children's librarians in academic and public libraries was $35,000 in 1995; catalogers and classifiers earned $36,300; and department heads earned $42,000. Library directors had an average salary of $58,200. Beginning librarians with a master's degree but no professional experience averaged $28,300 in 1995.

According to the Educational Research Service, experienced librarians in public schools averaged about $40,400 during the 1994–95 school year.

According to the Special Libraries Association, 1994 salaries for special librarians with two years or less of library experience averaged $31,100, and those with three to five years of experience averaged $35,200. Salaries for special librarians with primarily administrative responsibilities averaged $54,600.

Salaries for medical librarians with one year or less experience averaged $25,300 in 1994, according to the Medical Library

Association. The average salary for all medical librarians was $38,000.

The average annual salary for all librarians in the federal government in nonsupervisory, supervisory, and managerial positions was $48,200 in 1995.

Archivists

Archivists with a master's degree can expect to start out in the mid to high twenties. Someone with ten years under his or her belt working as an archivist with administrative responsibilities might earn $60,000 a year or more.

Salaries in the federal government depend upon education and experience. In 1995, inexperienced archivists with a bachelor's degree started at about $18,700, while those with some experience started at $23,200. Those with a master's degree typically started at $28,300 and with a doctorate, $34,300 to $41,100. In 1995, the average annual salary for archivists employed by the federal government in nonsupervisory, supervisory, and managerial positions was $50,000 a year.

What It's Really Like

Steve Oserman, Reference Librarian

Steve Oserman is a reference librarian in the Adult Services Department with the Skokie Public Library in Illinois. He has more than thirty years of combined teaching and library experience. He is coauthor of *The Guide to Internet Job Searching* with Margaret Riley and Frances Roehm, and he developed two books through the Job and Career Information Services Committee of the Public Library Association called *The Basic Guide to Resume Writing* and *The Basic Guide to Cover Letter Writing*.

"The way we have the day set up now I'm on the reference desk two hours, off two hours," Steve explains. "At the desk, I'm helping people with general reference questions on a variety of topics. I also assist people with the Internet and CD-ROMs. We have the Internet out for the public. When I'm off the desk, I run the employment resource center here. I have appointments to help patrons with resumes, job changes, Internet job search strategies, whatever help they need.

"We are especially aggressive in this area, and, in addition to the position I hold with the library, I'm the cochair of job and career information services for the Public Library Association. So I'm doing national speaking and training to help librarians develop their expertise in helping people find jobs and start career centers.

"I also do book discussions, and I do a lot of lectures and programs. I have seventeen programs coming up in the next twenty days. Most of them involve Internet job searching, but I also do things on dreams and health and healing for hospitals in the area. I'm also doing one for Motorola on financial resources on the Internet.

"I also trade options and do lectures on technical analysis of stock option trends. In addition, I do Chinese astrology and I Ching, and I always tell people to pursue at least seven careers simultaneously. I'm trying to have at least fourteen.

"I like my work a lot, but I don't like meetings and the bureaucratic paperwork. I like things that involve people. I'm very extroverted, and I like helping people find jobs or motivation. And I enjoy the seminars and public speaking I do.

"I'm here officially thirty-seven and a half hours a week, but I spend a lot more time than that. I come in early, and I come in in the evenings, too. I do my committee work on my days off."

Steve Oserman's Background

Steve Oserman has a B.S. in mathematics and philosophy from the University of Illinois at Champaign-Urbana and substantial work toward a Ph.D. in philosophy at Southern Illinois University at Carbondale, where he also taught philosophy.

"I'm atypical; I never went to library school. I started at a time when there was a shortage of librarians and got my training on the job. Plus, because I had more than two hundred credits of graduate work in other fields, my employers considered that as good as at least one year of library school.

"I started out with library work because it was a way to help finance my college education. It wasn't really a career I chose to go into. I was unhappy in the early years when I was doing more of the traditional librarian work, but I don't feel as stuck as I used to. Ever since I got more involved with career information areas it's been much more interesting."

Some Advice from Steve Oserman

"This career is not just being around books; it's really being around people much more. A lot of people think they might be a good candidate for a library job just because they like to be around books, but, actually, that's exactly what's not needed. There is probably a too high percentage of introverted people who are already in the library profession, as compared to the general population. We need more extroverted people.

"There are still lots of jobs available, especially in the Midwest, compared with other jobs I've checked into, but it's not very good on the East and West Coasts, where libraries are closing, and in the South. You might have to be prepared to relocate to find the best job.

"I think that it's a profession that a lot of people in it love the work they do. At seminars I've had for librarians I've been surprised at how many of them really do enjoy their work. The only problem is a lot of them would like to have more career development possibilities. A lot of librarians plateau where there's not enough room for advancement. This should be taken into consideration when choosing this career."

Carol Jones, Technical Services and Interlibrary Loan Librarian

Carol Jones works at the Kline Science Library, one of many libraries at Yale University in New Haven, Connecticut. She has been a librarian for more than twenty years.

"Technical services is a broad term that includes acquisitions and cataloging and binding of materials. My position is very similar to working in a business. Acquisitions means we buy materials—books and electronic resources. We have a lot of journals that are now available in an electronic format over the Internet, as opposed to being printed on paper and bound in a cover.

"The budget we have for buying materials is over $1 million, so this is big business. Once we order those materials, we have to see that they're received and made available on the shelves. My position is administrative, and I supervise four people, monitor budgets, write policies and procedures, and train people. I meet with vendors, the people from whom we buy various materials, and work on problems. I also serve on committees in the university library that have to work with a wide range of issues.

"Right now a good deal of my time is also spent working with computers and the hardware and software side of things. We have a local area network, and we have work stations for all of our staff and for the patrons. I do a lot of the work myself, and I also coordinate the computer work for the five other science libraries at Yale.

"I like the detail of it and the business orientation of it. I never really wanted to go into the corporate world. Academe does have nice benefits in terms of vacation time and a certain flexibility I think would be missing in a corporate setting.

"From what I've heard from friends who work in public libraries, I think I'd much prefer the university setting I'm in. The patrons are very different. The public libraries deal with current readings, they have children and adults with a real wide range of interests. We have students and faculty who are fairly focused.

"There is a considerable amount of pressure and stress with my job, though. We're not unlike many businesses right now in which there is an increasing emphasis on downsizing, resource reallocation, greater productivity with few people, and that takes a toll.

"Also, the technology, which is an integral part of what we do, is changing so fast, there are times when I feel I haven't even learned one thing and it's already time to go on to the next generation after that."

Carol Jones's Background

Carol Jones earned her B.A. in history from Kentucky Wesleyan and her M.L.S. from the University of Kentucky in Lexington in the School of Library and Information Science. She worked for nine years at the library at Kentucky Wesleyan, then went to Yale in 1983 as a government documents librarian.

"I got interested in library work when I was an undergraduate, but I was rather an old undergraduate. I was already married and had three children before I started college. My interest stemmed mainly from my own use of the library, but I didn't pursue it until my last year in college, when I started working part-time in the library.

"Part of it was a love for books and an interest in publishing, information, and research. But also I did take some undergraduate classes in library science, and though many people might have found cataloging of materials and organizing materials so they could be found with ease terribly boring, it was of great interest to me.

"Also, on a more practical level, perhaps, it offered an opportunity for a career that had a certain amount of flexibility, which was particularly important to me at that point since I did have young children.

"After that I decided to get a master's degree because I knew I wouldn't make any money unless I did that."

Some Advice from Carol Jones

"If anything, the field of librarianship is going to become even more interesting and more important as electronic resources are more broadly available. As information expands and expands at an ever faster rate, librarians are going to be integral in making that information understandable and accessible to the people who need some piece of it. It's one thing to say everyone will have a computer and they'll be able to do it all themselves. But in actuality, someone who is familiar with the way the information is organized and how you can get at it is going to be crucial. And that someone is going to be a librarian. Knowledge of computers and information resources is absolutely essential.

"Subject expertise and language expertise has always been useful, too, and it will be even more so in the future."

John Fleckner, Chief Archivist, National Museum of American History, Smithsonian Institution

John Fleckner came to the Smithsonian in 1982 with more than a decade's experience working as an archivist for the State Historical Society of Wisconsin. He is a past president of the Society of American Archivists and has acted as a consultant on many important archives projects including the United Negro College Fund, the Vietnam History and Archives Project, and the Native American Archives Project.

"Archivists provide a service to society by identifying and preserving materials with lasting value for the future," he explains. "When archivists talk about their work, they discuss certain basic functions that are common to all archives.

"I oversee a professional staff of twelve archivists, three student interns, and close to twenty volunteers. About 50 percent of my time is spent in supervision. The rest covers the identification and acquisition of materials; providing reference services;

handling administrative duties—meetings, budget, personnel; then there's outreach and public affairs.

"The archives I am responsible for acquires collections from the outside and does not handle the records generated by the museum. The collections cover a wide range of subjects and are particularly strong in the areas of American music, advertising, and the history of technology.

"As with libraries and archives, there are distinct differences between librarians and archivists, the way they operate, and the methods and techniques they use to handle material.

"The biggest single difference is that librarians look at materials they get on an item-by-item basis. Each book is a distinct entity evaluated separately from the other books. In an archives, a single letter would usually be part of a larger collection of letters. Archivists are interested in these as a group, because one letter would only be a fragment. To really understand something about the past, the information needs to be synthesized and put together to form a collection."

John Fleckner's Background

John Fleckner did his undergraduate work at Colgate, in Hamilton, New York, graduating in 1963 with a B.A. with honors in history. He earned his M.A. in American history at the University of Wisconsin in 1965 and also has amassed significant work toward his Ph.D.

"After too many years of graduate school, pursuing a vague notion of teaching college-level history, I realized that I really didn't want to teach. I was so naive, it took a university career counselor to recognize that my history background might be anything other than an economic liability. Leaning back in her chair, she pointed out her office window to the State Historical Society of Wisconsin just across the street, and she directed me to a recently established graduate program in archives administration. The instructor would make no promises about the prospects for a job, but, with a sly smile, he offered that all his previous students were working. I didn't need a weatherman—as they said in those days, the early 1970s—to tell me which way the wind was blowing.

"So, it was an accident in good guidance that got me in the door. But it was the experience of doing archival work—beginning with the simplest class exercises and then a formal internship—that sealed it for me. I loved the combination of handicraft and analytical work and I loved the intense, intimate contact with the stuff of history. Before I completed my internship, I knew I wanted to be an archivist.

"Previously, as a graduate student, of course I had done some research in archives—at the Library of Congress, the College of William and Mary, and especially the State Historical Society. But the archivists had taken all the fun out of it—the materials were antiseptically foldered, boxed, and listed. Wheeled out on carts, they were like cadavers to be dissected by first-year medical students. On occasion, I even donned white gloves. The documents always seemed lifeless.

"Later, as a would-be archivist, they thrilled me. I was in charge; I would evaluate the significance of the materials, determine their order, describe their contents, and physically prepare them for their permanent resting places. Still, it was not so much this heady feeling of control that awed me but more the mystery, the possibilities of the records themselves. My judgments would be critical to building paths to the records for generations of researchers, across the entire spectrum of topics, and into unknown future time.

"The archival enterprise held another attractive feature for me. For all the opportunity to reconstruct the past captured in these documents, and to imagine the future research they might support, I had a well-defined task to accomplish, a product to produce, techniques and methods for proceeding, and standards against which my work would be judged. There was rigor and discipline; this was real work. And, as good fortune would have it, I soon was getting paid to do it."

Some Advice from John Fleckner

"People get into the archives profession in a variety of traditional and unusual ways. Often in a small town an archives is a closet in the back room of a local historical society's office. Someone volunteers to put it all together, perhaps the oldest person in the community with a strong interest in the area's history.

"But to assure a professional, paid position, I'd recommend you pursue either a degree in history with specific archives courses or a master's degree in library science with courses in archives administration."

CHAPTER FOUR

Freelance Researchers

R esearch—in a variety of subject areas—is a major interest of most scholars and a large component of many of
the jobs covered in this book. University professors, curators, archivists, and anthropologists, to name just a few, involve
themselves in some way with research activity. In this chapter
you will learn about genealogy as a career and also be introduced
to several researchers whose jobs don't fall into any of the
expected categories.

Genealogists

The study of genealogy, tracing family histories, has recently
become one of the most popular hobbies in the United States.
Most everyone has a keen interest in their family backgrounds.
Many genealogy hobbyists take their interest one step further
and become self-employed genealogists, helping others to dig up
their family trees. Genealogists also are employed in historical
societies and libraries with special genealogy rooms.

The Church of Jesus Christ of Latter-Day Saints in Salt Lake
City, for example, has a huge repository of family information in
a subterranean library. The church employs genealogists all over
the world and includes genealogists who have been accredited
through their own program on a list of freelance researchers. For
more information write to:

Accreditation Program, Family History Library
35 Northwest Temple Street
Salt Lake City, UT 84150

Other genealogists find work teaching their skills to others in adult education classes or by editing genealogy magazines or writing books or newspaper genealogy columns.

Most genealogists are not formally trained, though specializing in genealogy is possible through some university history and library science programs. In addition, a genealogist can become board certified. For information on certification requirements and procedures write to:

Board for Certification of Genealogists
P.O. Box 5816
Falmouth, VA 22403

Salaries

Salaries vary depending upon the institution where a genealogist is employed and upon the level of expertise he or she has reached. Self-employed genealogists make anywhere from $15 to $35 an hour.

How to Get Started

The National Genealogy Society makes the following suggestions for beginners:

1. *Question older family members.* Encourage them to talk about their childhoods and relatives and listen carefully for clues they might inadvertently drop. Learn good interviewing techniques so you ask questions that elicit the most

productive answers. Use a tape recorder and try to verify each fact through a separate source.

2. *Visit your local library.* Become familiar with historical and genealogical publications (a few sources are provided at the end of this chapter and in the Appendix) and contact local historical societies and the state library and archives in your state capital. Seek out any specialty ethnic or religious libraries and visit cemeteries.

3. *Visit courthouses.* Cultivate friendships with busy court clerks. Ask to see source records such as wills, deeds, marriage books, birth and death certificates.

4. *Enter into correspondence.* Write to other individuals or societies involved with the same families or regions. Contact foreign embassies in Washington, D.C. Restrict yourself to asking only one question in each letter you send. Include the information you have already uncovered. Include a self-addressed stamped envelope to encourage replies.

5. *Become computer literate.* Members of the National Genealogical Society can participate in a special computer interest section. It encourages the use of computers in research, record management, and data sharing.

6. *Keep painstaking records.* Use printed family group sheets or pedigree charts. Develop a well-organized filing system so you'll be able to easily find your information. Keep separate records for each family you research.

7. *Write the National Genealogical Society.* Take advantage of the society's forty-six-page book, *Beginners in Genealogy,* charts, and library loan program. You can also enroll in the basic home-study course, American Genealogy.

What It's Really Like

Valarie Neiman, Academic Researcher

Valarie Neiman formed EVN Flow Services in 1993. Through her home-based business, she does academic, business, and creative writing and provides research and editing services.

She earned her B.S. in business administration (transportation) in 1980 from Arizona State University in Tempe and her M.A. in human resources development in 1993 from Ottawa University in Phoenix.

"Research isn't what I do, it's part of who I am," Valerie explains. "As one of the original latchkey kids in the 1950s, I spent a lot of time reading when I got home from school. To avoid being bored in class, I'd always read ahead in the textbooks. My first job fresh out of high school in 1966 was typing resumes. Surprising how little they've changed in thirty years. The woman I worked for began letting me write them, and, soon, I did the interviews as well.

"After a variety of clerical and secretarial jobs, I went back to school in my mid-twenties and earned a bachelor's degree in business. Eventually, while working for a major defense contractor, I began work on a master's. I was excused from the employer who had been paying my tuition and went on to temporary positions—from management consultant back to typist. Bummer!

"My final temp assignment was researching and writing warehouse procedures. I convinced the manager that it would be cheaper to hire me as an independent contractor rather than pay the temp agency. At the same time, I put up a notice at my alma mater offering to help students with their research projects.

"The rest, as they say, is history. When I began EVN Flow (Ellwood and Valarie Neiman keep work flowing), my current business, I expected to help students format and type their papers. However, adult learners (twenty-five and older) often haven't had training or don't remember how to write research papers. My work soon evolved into filling in the gaps in their abilities. Part of the job is reassuring them that they aren't stupid, letting them know I've developed a unique (and marketable) talent for pulling their work together into a package that makes them look good.

"The work I do is enjoyable because every day is different and every project takes me on a new path. Had I realized years ago that I am what is gently referred to as an individual contributor, I may have found my niche sooner. I prefer to work alone, without supervision. I focus on the task at hand and am goal oriented enough to get it done so I can move to the next project.

"People may think of researchers as scientists or academics. I believe research is an element in almost every job, whether dealing with things, people, or ideas. Most of the time, though, it isn't thought of as research.

"To me, the distinction of a job as a researcher is that the goal is to present knowledge in a different way, consolidate facts and assemble them to make a point, discover new relationships in existing knowledge, or develop background and authenticity—in creative writing, for example.

"One of the things I like least about my work is that it isn't full-time and can be seasonal. I began writing a novel to fill those dreaded unbillable hours. Of course, the part-time nature of the work is also one of the things I like best! I'm sure that others in various types of research positions make a living. By my own choice, I make enough to pay business expenses and to pay myself a small stipend. Because I am a business, travel, postage, supplies, and capital equipment associated with my writing are all considered expenses.

"My business is home based. I have one employee (my husband), who is financial manager and gofer. We share a large office and one mother-ship computer, and I have an old laptop for plain old writing.

"I tutor adult learners in planning, researching, and writing academic papers. I edit master's research and graduation review projects. I am under contract with Ottawa University to read and edit first drafts of master's candidates' theses.

"I also collaborate on research and writing a series of booklets on pricing, niche marketing, networking, outsourcing, tax tips, and how to start a home-based business (published by the Home-Based Business Association of Arizona, HBBA).

"My time is mine to spend as I wish. Since I like variety, and big projects, I find I work for an hour or so on one, then shift to another, and so forth. Some days, I catch up on phone calls or maintenance, but if I have paying clients, I stay focused on them. Some days I work fourteen hours (rare), others only three or four. I have a wonderful, understanding boss."

Some Advice from Valarie Neiman

"Read, read, read, research, research, research. Go to the library, get on-line, practice finding things. Interview people, create questionnaires, read magazines.

"The key requirement for a life of research is a desire, not to say compulsion, to *know*. In addition, a researcher (whether scientific, academic, or journalistic) needs persistence, judgment, empathy, and intuition. A researcher must establish limits and develop shortcuts or the process goes on forever, each step leading to another source, ad infinitum.

"A researcher with broad experience is more likely to be exposed to a variety of sources—not just the public library. I've worked in government, major corporations, and small businesses. Each job provided a whole new set of resources that I am now able to draw upon.

"How to get a research job? The possibilities are endless, but chances are good there won't be an ad in the newspaper. Researcher is more an activity than a job title. It's the same old story. Network, create an excellent resume, and research your prospects.

"A college degree or three is probably a good start (up to and including a Ph.D. or postdoctoral experience). The academic major doesn't matter. A student who thrives in an academic environment will likely have the curiosity and temperament to excel as a researcher.

"With the emphasis on education (to keep youngsters out of the job market as long as possible), even a fact checker at a newspaper or magazine would probably need a degree.

"Hone those writing skills. Research is useless without presenting results. Facts are just data. A researcher worth his or her salt must be able to interpret the facts and consolidate or extrapolate them into usable information.

"And remember, in scientific or social research, especially, the honesty and ethics of a researcher must be unquestioned. A researcher must maintain the confidentiality of people and ideas."

Susan Broadwater-Chen, Information Specialist and Freelance Writer

Susan Broadwater-Chen owns Moonstone Research and Publications, her own home-based business in Charlottesville, Virginia. She has a bachelor's degree in humanities from Asbury College in Wilmore, Kentucky, and her master's in theological studies from Emory University in Atlanta, Georgia.

"I have an insatiable curiosity about just about everything, and I love to write," she says. "I especially like the challenge of having to find something and the excitement that comes when I find it. I love libraries, books, and puzzles, and some of the searches that I do are very much like putting puzzles together.

"I attended Mountain Empire Community College in Southwest Virginia in the early 1980s and took as many computer courses, including programming, as were offered. After finishing those courses, I took a job at the University of Virginia (UVA) as a program support technician, and part of my job was to do a lot of editing and spend time working with research assistants.

"Eventually I took courses through UVA on how to navigate the Internet and do web pages. I worked at UVA for ten years and ran a business out of my home doing everything from research to editing during that time.

"I started in 1986 on a part-time, moonlighting basis. I've been full-time since 1995. I had built up enough contacts and customers that I could become independent, and I quit my job at UVA and started publishing a monthly newsletter and running a web page. When I realized that I could support myself by using my skills to expand my client base, I decided to devote myself full-time to this business.

"Currently I publish a monthly newsletter that focuses on Internet materials that writers will find useful. I also take individual research projects from authors who are looking for information that is proving hard for them to find on their own.

"In addition, I work with a couple of on-line author colonies or work groups in developing content for research libraries. This includes going through antiquarian books, microfilm, and other sources to provide both primary source materials and bibliographical information. My company has a storefront on the Internet where writers or anyone else can download some materials for free and pay for others. I offer a clipping service for subscribers and hold a weekly workshop on-line to help people with any questions they might have about finding what they are looking for.

"The job is very demanding. Most of my customers can't wait a week or two for what they are looking for. In addition, putting out a large newsletter each month and submitting articles to at least one on-line magazine each month is very time consuming. I begin my day at 6 A.M. and, as my son eats his breakfast, I check my E-mail, writing down every request that comes through on a special pad. After that, I check the newsgroups and news services to see if there is anything I need to come back to later and delete what I don't want to look at. After I get my son on the bus, I come back and print the articles I want to read or save. As soon as that is done, I file them in topical folders. You have to be organized in this job or you are doomed to have all kinds of paper and not know how to put your hands on what you really need when you need it. I keep a folder of things I may want to review or talk about in my newsletter, and the rest is filed by topic. Next I work on the products I intend to sell. This means reading and writing articles or finding out of copyright primary source material that can be edited and reprinted for sale. I try to do a minimum number of these products a day. After that is finished, I turn to the content I am developing for the on-line services.

"When that is finished, it's time to check E-mail again and to start working on the requests I have received overnight. I walk after that because I need time to myself and away from my desk. When I come back to work, I write at least one review or article for my newsletter and then start exploring potential Internet sources that I may want to review. I take notes and make printouts and put this aside to be written up the next day. Next I Telnet into library card catalogs looking for materials that I may want to request on interlibrary loan from my local library and write down information on those books.

"Because I work at home it's a relaxed atmosphere, but sometimes I feel really pressured because there seems to be so much to do and only a limited number of hours in a day. I usually work about eighty hours a week, which is forty more than when I worked for someone else. I have one morning that I spend in the library every week. The job is not boring, but it's not easy money either.

"I like it when I can help somebody, and it makes me feel good to know that they are happy with what I've found for them. When I've helped a person who is publishing books and he or she sends me a copy of the book, I get personal satisfaction knowing that I've helped them with the research that the book required. I also like the feeling I get when I find some really obscure fact and pull the needle out of the haystack. The downside is that sometimes I can't help someone because the facts won't bear out what they want to write about."

Some Advice from Susan Broadwater-Chen

"It's not an easy job. You need to learn all you can about electronic databases and the Internet. In addition, you need to learn all you can about how to find information in your library and from interviewing people.

"You can't have a business based on doing Internet research alone. You have to cultivate as many skills as possible and know where to look for specific material. It's also important to build up a client base and connections before you take this on full-time. Volunteer to do things for groups who might need your services on the Internet and on-line services. Submit articles to on-line publications and start networking with people in professions or with interests who might need your services."

CHAPTER FIVE

Social Scientists

S ocial scientists study all aspects of human society, from the distribution of goods and services to the beliefs of newly formed religious groups to modern mass transportation systems. Social science research provides insights that help us understand the different ways in which individuals and groups make decisions, exercise power, or respond to change. Through their studies and analyses, social scientists assist educators, government officials, business leaders, and others in solving social, economic, and environmental problems.

Research is a basic activity for many social scientists. They use established or newly discovered methods to assemble facts and theory that contribute to human knowledge. Applied research usually is designed to produce information that will enable people to make better decisions or manage their affairs more effectively. Interviews and surveys are widely used to collect facts, opinions, or other information. Data collection takes many other forms, however, including living and working among the people studied; archaeological and other field investigations; the analysis of historical records and documents; experiments with human subjects or animals in a psychological laboratory; the administration of standardized tests and questionnaires; and the preparation and interpretation of maps and graphic materials.

Social sciences are interdisciplinary in nature. Specialists in one field often find that the research they are performing overlaps work that is being conducted in another social science discipline. Regardless of their fields of specialization, social scientists are concerned with some aspect of society, culture, or personality.

Anthropologists study the origin and the physical, social, and cultural development and behavior of humans. They may study the way of life, remains, language, or physical characteristics of people in various parts of the world; they compare the customs, values, and social patterns of different cultures. Anthropologists generally concentrate in sociocultural anthropology, archaeology, linguistics, or biological-physical anthropology.

Sociocultural anthropologists study the customs, cultures, and social lives of groups in a wide range of settings from nonindustrialized societies to modern urban cultures.

Archaeology is a subdivision of the field of anthropology. *Archaeologists* study the artifacts of past cultures to learn about their histories, customs, and living habits. They survey and excavate archaeological sites, recording and cataloging their finds. By careful analysis, archaeologists reconstruct earlier cultures and determine their influences on the present.

Archaeological sites are the physical remains of past civilizations. They can include building debris and the items found inside, in addition to trash and garbage. Usually these sites have been buried by other, later human activity or by natural processes. Excavation of these sites is a painstaking process conducted by professionals using modern techniques. Because these sites are so fragile, the very nature of excavating destroys some information. With this in mind, archaeologists are careful to dig only as much as they need to answer important questions.

Frequently, archaeologists concentrate their work on sites slated to be destroyed for highway or new building construction.

Linguistic anthropologists study the role of language in various cultures.

Biological-physical anthropologists study the evolution of the human body and look for the earliest evidences of human life.

Economists study the production, distribution, and consumption of commodities and services. They may conduct surveys and analyze data to determine public preferences for these goods and services. Most economists are concerned with the practical applications of economic policy in a particular area, such as finance, labor, agriculture, transportation, energy, or health.

Others develop theories to explain economic phenomena such as unemployment or inflation.

Marketing research analysts research market conditions in localities, regions, the nation, or the world to determine potential sales of a product or service; they examine and analyze data on past sales and trends to develop forecasts.

Geographers study the distribution of both physical and cultural phenomena on local, regional, continental, and global scales. Geographers specialize, as a rule. (Some occupational classification systems include geographers under physical scientists rather than social scientists.)

Economic geographers study the regional distribution of resources and economic activities. *Political geographers* are concerned with the relationship of geography to political phenomena at local, national, and international levels.

Physical geographers study the distribution of climates, vegetation, soil, and land forms.

Urban and transportation geographers study cities and metropolitan areas, while *regional geographers* study the physical, climatic, economic, political, and cultural characteristics of regions, ranging in size from a congressional district to a state, country, continent, or the entire world.

Medical geographers study health care delivery systems, epidemiology, and the effect of the environment on health.

Geographic Information Systems (GIS) analysts work in a specialty that combines computer graphics, artificial intelligence, and high-speed communication to store, retrieve, manipulate, analyze, and map geographic data. GIS is widely used in weather forecasting, emergency management, resource analysis and management, and other activities.

Historians research and analyze the past. (See Chapters 3 and 7 for close-ups of an archivist and a history museum curator.) They use many information sources in their research, including government and institutional records, newspapers and other periodicals, photographs, interviews, films, and unpublished manuscripts such as diaries and letters. Historians usually specialize in a specific country or region; in a particular time period; or in a particular field, such as social, intellectual, political, or diplomatic history. Biographers collect detailed information on individuals.

Genealogists trace family histories (see Chapter 4). Other historians help study and preserve archival materials, artifacts, and historic buildings and sites.

Political scientists study the origin, development, and operation of political systems. They conduct research on a wide range of subjects, such as relations between the United States and foreign countries, the beliefs and institutions of foreign nations (for example, those in Asia and Africa), the politics of small towns or a major metropolis, or the decisions of the U.S. Supreme Court.

Studying topics such as public opinion, political decision making, and ideology, they analyze the structure and operation of governments as well as informal political entities. Depending on the topic, a political scientist might conduct a public opinion survey, analyze election results, or analyze public documents.

Psychologists, who constitute more than half of all social scientists, study human behavior and counsel or advise individuals or groups. Their research also assists business advertisers, politicians, and others interested in influencing or motivating people. While clinical psychology is the largest specialty, psychologists specialize in many other fields, such as counseling, experimental, social, or industrial psychology. (See Chapter 6 for a more detailed look at the psychology profession.)

Sociologists analyze the development, structure, and behavior of groups or social systems such as families, neighborhoods, or clubs. Sociologists may specialize in a particular field, such as criminology, rural sociology, or medical sociology.

Urban and regional planners develop comprehensive plans and programs for the use of land for industrial and public sites. Planners prepare for situations that are likely to develop as a result of population growth or social and economic change.

Working Conditions

Most social scientists have regular hours. Generally working behind a desk, either alone or in collaboration with other social scientists, they read and write research reports. Often they experience the pressures of deadlines and tight schedules, and sometimes they must work overtime, for which they generally are not reimbursed.

Social scientists often work as an integral part of a research team. The routine may be interrupted frequently by telephone calls, letters to answer, special requests for information, meetings, or conferences.

Travel may be necessary to collect information or attend meetings. Social scientists on foreign assignment must adjust to unfamiliar cultures and climates.

Some social scientists do fieldwork. For example, anthropologists, archaeologists, and geographers often must travel to remote areas, live among the people they study, and stay for long periods at the site of their investigations. They may work under primitive conditions, and their work may involve strenuous physical exertion.

Social scientists employed by colleges and universities usually have flexible work schedules, often dividing their time among teaching, research, consulting, or administrative responsibilities.

Employment Options

Social scientists held about 259,000 jobs in 1994. More than half of all social scientists are psychologists. About one-third of all social scientists are self-employed and involved in counseling, consulting, or research.

Salaried social scientists work for a wide range of employers. Nearly four out of ten are employed with federal, state, and local governments; three out of ten work in health, research, and management services firms; and two out of ten social scientists work in educational institutions as researchers, administrators, and counselors.

Other employers include social service agencies, international organizations, associations, museums, historical societies, computer and data processing firms, and business firms.

In addition, many persons with training in a social science discipline teach in colleges and universities (see Chapter 2) and in secondary and elementary schools.

The proportion of social scientists who teach varies by occupation. For example, the academic world generally is a more important source of jobs for graduates in sociology than for graduates in psychology.

Training

Educational attainment of social scientists is among the highest of all occupations. The Ph.D. or an equivalent degree is a minimum requirement for most positions in colleges and universities and is important for advancement to many top-level nonacademic research and administrative posts.

Graduates with master's degrees generally have better professional opportunities outside of colleges and universities, although the situation varies by field. For example, job prospects for master's degree holders in urban or regional planning are brighter than for master's degree holders in history.

Graduates with a master's degree in a social science discipline qualify for teaching positions in junior colleges. Bachelor's degree holders have limited opportunities and in most social science occupations do not qualify for professional positions.

The bachelor's degree does, however, provide a suitable background for many different kinds of entry-level jobs, such as research assistant, administrative aide, or management trainee.

With the addition of sufficient education courses, social science graduates also can qualify for teaching positions in secondary and elementary schools. Training in statistics and mathematics is essential for many social scientists. Mathematical and other quantitative research methods are increasingly used in economics, geography, political science, experimental psychology, and other fields. The ability to use computers for research purposes is mandatory in most disciplines.

Depending on their jobs, social scientists and urban planners may need a wide range of personal characteristics. Because they constantly seek new information about people, things, and ideas, intellectual curiosity and creativity are fundamental personal traits. The ability to think logically and methodically is important to a political scientist comparing the merits of various forms of government. The ability to analyze data is important to an economist studying proposals to reduce federal budget deficits. Objectivity, open-mindedness, and systematic work habits are important in all kinds of social science research.

Perseverance is essential for an anthropologist, who might spend years accumulating artifacts from an ancient civilization. Emotional stability and sensitivity are vital to a clinical psychologist working with mental patients. Written and oral communication skills are essential to all these workers.

Job Outlook

Employment of social scientists is expected to grow faster than the average for all occupations through the year 2005, spurred by rising concern over the environment, crime, communicable diseases, mental illness, the growing elderly and homeless populations, the increasingly competitive global economy, and a wide range of other issues. Psychology, the largest social science occupation, is expected to grow much faster than average. Economists and marketing research analysts, urban and regional planners, and all other social scientists combined, including anthropologists, geographers, historians, political scientists, and sociologists, should experience average growth.

Most job openings, however, will result from the need to replace social scientists who transfer to other occupations or stop working altogether.

Prospects are best for those with advanced degrees and generally are better in disciplines such as economics, psychology, and urban and regional planning, which offer many opportunities in nonacademic settings.

However, graduates in all social science fields are expected to find enhanced job opportunities in applied fields due to the excellent research, communication, and quantitative skills they develop in school. Government agencies, health and social service organizations, marketing, research, and consulting firms, and a wide range of businesses seek social science graduates.

Social scientists currently face stiff competition for academic positions. However, competition may ease in the future due to a wave of retirements expected among college and university faculty. The growing importance and popularity of social science subjects in secondary schools is strengthening the demand for social science teachers at this level as well.

Other considerations that affect employment opportunities in these occupations include specific skills and technical expertise, desired work setting, salary requirements, and geographic mobility. In addition, experience acquired through internships can prove invaluable later in obtaining a full-time position in a social science field.

Salaries

Median annual earnings of all social scientists were approximately $38,000 in 1994. The middle 50 percent earned between

$23,200 and $52,600 annually. The lowest 10 percent earned less than $17,300, while the highest 10 percent earned more than $70,800.

According to a 1995 survey by the National Association of Colleges and Employers, people with a bachelor's degree in a social science field received starting offers averaging about $22,000 a year in 1995. Those with a master's degree in a social science field received starting offers averaging about $29,500 a year in 1995, and the average salary offer for doctoral social scientists was $33,000.

In the federal government, social scientists with a bachelor's degree and no experience could start at $18,700 or $23,200 a year in 1995, depending on their college records. Those with a master's degree could start at $28,300, and those having a doctoral degree could begin at $34,300, while some individuals with experience and an advanced degree could start at $41,100.

The average salary of all social scientists working for the federal government in nonsupervisory, supervisory, and managerial positions in 1995 was about $45,230 in geography; $51,180 in history; $56,780 in sociology; and $38,770 in archaeology.

Social scientists entering careers in higher education may receive benefits such as summer research money, computer access, student research assistants, and secretarial support.

What It's Really Like

Ann Gardner, Social Anthropologist

Ann Gardner is a social anthropologist who has done extensive fieldwork in the Middle East, especially working with Bedouin women in the Sinai Desert. She earned her B.A. in anthropology in 1982 from Friends World College (Jerusalem Center). She studied Arabic from 1983 to 1985 at the American University in

Cairo and received her M.A. in anthropology in 1987 from the University of Texas at Austin. She also earned her Ph.D. (1994) in anthropology from the University of Texas at Austin.

"All that education, and over six years of living in the Middle East," Ann Gardner explains, "resulted in a 483-page dissertation, 'Women and Changing Relations in a South Sinai Bedouin Community' (1994)."

Ann Gardner's Background

"As corny as it sounds, as a young child, I named a stuffed toy 'Journey,' because I was going to take him with me on all my travels. So, I have almost always been interested in other places. My inspiration was likely in part the nightly bedtime stories my mother read me, but I also just seemed to know my path in life.

"A decade or so passed, with increasingly little more thought given to my initial interests, but then, almost as an aside, I took some anthropological area studies in high school that renewed my interest.

"My career as an anthropologist started in 1978. My undergraduate major was anthropology, as were my graduate degrees. I went to a college with centers around the world that stressed cross-cultural experience, so I had far more field experience than most graduate students.

"Most large university anthropology graduate departments offer programs in social/cultural anthropology, economic anthropology, physical anthropology, linguistics, folklore, archaeology, museum studies, and, sometimes, development anthropology. Some of these specializations overlap to certain degrees. The professors will have regional expertise in the various geographical regions. You may also take classes from other departments.

"Before entering graduate school to study anthropology, you should have decided upon your specialization. You will be required to take core classes covering the various specializations as a graduate student, but generally the more you have done at the undergraduate level towards your interest, the better your chances are of getting into graduate school. Most students also already know which world regions they are interested in, too.

"You have to have, or quickly learn, many skills to be a successful graduate anthropology student. You should be able to perform very well academically, which usually means not taking incompletes and not getting more than one B. Where I went to graduate school, UT-Austin, it was not uncommon to have to read around five hundred, often dense, pages a week, per class. Most full-time graduate students took three courses a semester, while some took four.

"You need to be able to write theoretically for an academic audience and also still be able to write well for the general public, if that is your interest. You need to have grant-writing skills, as detailed above. If you are working as a teaching assistant, you will likely need to have course-development and teaching skills. As a TA, you will also need rapid grading skills, because you will often have at least several hundred exams and essays to read at once, usually at the same time that your own papers and exams are due. You need to be able to do research, which, for anthropologists, often includes living in another culture while doing cross-cultural fieldwork.

"Anthropology is a very diversified field, which has the potential to 'grow' with your evolving interests. As an undergraduate social anthropology student researching Sinai Bedouin women, my initial attraction to the field was my interest in other cultures and an interest in promoting international understanding. Over the years, I saw the Bedouins become increasingly marginalized by 'development.' So I became interested in that subfield of anthropology as well, for anthropologists are in a good position to help voice the concerns of people and help access the possibilities for change. I was personally disappointed, however, to find that the main focus in the discipline of anthropology was often with theoretical postmodern debates, though that may be changing.

"If you are interested in majoring in anthropology for your B.A., I strongly recommend that you go to a good college that offers anthropology, rather than to a large university where you will likely get little personal attention.

"If you are interested in getting a job in anthropology, you usually need to go on to graduate school. Graduate training in anthropology is an enormous commitment, both time- and money-wise. Ten years is currently about the average for getting an M.A. and Ph.D. Even if you are willing to make that sort of time commitment, you must think long and hard about the financial reality of going to graduate school. I was lucky to have been offered teaching assistantships from my first semester and to have had numerous grants and the support of my parents, but that is unusual. Many students have to work outside of the school and/or have to start paying back huge student loans upon graduation.

"It is very important to take fellowship and grant writing classes early on, as it is a vital skill for anthropologists, who almost all need to do funded field research and writing. So far, I have received funding from the National Science Foundation, the Wenner-Gren Anthropological Society, the American Research Center in Egypt, and the Research and Exploration Committee of the National Geographic Society. I was also awarded a Fulbright-Hayes grant but activated others in its stead.

"Choose your graduate school, subspecialization, and potential graduate advisor very carefully. The main stress in graduate anthropology is academics, unless you select an applied program or have previous in-depth field experience to draw on. Many programs focus on training their students in postmodern theory and to become professors. Some programs that also offer museum and folklore studies may include training to get a museum position—a position that you may be able to get with an M.A.

"Currently, the competition is very steep for teaching positions. You almost always have to have a Ph.D. for a professorship or even a lecturer position. People marketing themselves for the teaching job market may do better if they can teach in more than one discipline. An anthropologist might get a job as a women's studies or religion professor, for example. It is not uncommon for an open position to have hundreds of applicants and for the starting salary of a new assistant professor to be only around $30,000. Some Ph.D.s take jobs as teachers in private high schools, which can be easier to secure and may pay more.

"If your interest is in applied anthropology and you want a full-time job at a development agency, government agency, or a non-government agency, then you also need to take management courses and secure intern positions with an agency as a student. A Ph.D. is best, but some positions can be obtained with a M.A.

"Other applied anthropologists do contract research. While that can be very, very unreliable, it is becoming more common for development agencies, for example, to want the input of anthropologists. I had focused on development as one of my specializations, and, even before I had formally graduated with my Ph.D., I was offered the possibility of working on a three-year Bedouin and development project in a region different from where I had done my previous research, but my first priority was to rewrite my dissertation into a book.

"Presently, I am writing more grant proposals and rewriting my dissertation for popular press publication. Most people publish their dissertations with an academic press, but I want to reach a wide audience: students, academics, development personal, and the general public.

"As a practicing anthropologist, I am continuing my interest in writing and field research. I receive income from professional writing, grants, and consulting contract work for development agencies, research organizations, and the like. But my current main focus is rewriting my dissertation into a book and articles to promote it. I also may teach some at a later date. Relying on money from contract work, research grants, and writing income is certainly risky, but I was never interested in being a full-time professor, even if the job market were good, which it isn't."

A Close-Up Look at Archaeology

Archaeologists work in a variety of settings. The following chart lists these settings and the duties specific to each.

Setting	Duties	Conditions
Universities and Colleges, Private Institutions	Teaching, Fieldwork, Research, Directing Student Fieldwork	Classroom, Labs, Office Space
Museums	Fieldwork, Research Classifying, Preserving, Displaying	Display and Research Areas, Office Space
Public Sector (local, state, and national government agencies)	Excavating, Surveying, Analyzing, Preserving, Recording Remains	On-site, Labs, Research Facilities
Private Sector (construction/ architectural firms)	Excavating, Surveying, Preserving, Recording Remains	On-site, Labs, Research Facilities

Archaeologists conducting fieldwork often work with several other professionals in a team effort. They are assisted by geologists, ethnologists, educators, anthropologists, ecologists, and aerial photographers.

In the field, archaeologists use a variety of tools during an excavation. These include picks, shovels, trowels, wheelbarrows, sifting boxes, pressure sprayers, and brushes. Archaeologists also make drawings and sketches on-site and take notes and photographs.

What It Takes to Become an Archaeologist

Do you have what it takes to become an archaeologist? Take this self-evaluation quiz and find out. Put a check mark under the appropriate heading.

	YES	NO
1. I have above average academic ability.	—	—
2. I have an avid interest in science and history.	—	—
3. Hours of strenuous activity (lifting, carrying, shoveling) do not pose a problem for me.	—	—
4. I have been told I have leadership qualities.	—	—
5. The idea of continuing study throughout my career appeals to me.	—	—
6. I am a logical and analytical thinker.	—	—
7. I enjoy working independently.	—	—
8. I function well as part of a team.	—	—
9. I believe professional ethics should be strictly adhered to.	—	—
10. I can live under primitive conditions in remote areas.	—	—

To consider yourself a potential archaeologist, you must have been able to check 'Yes' for every question. Even with just one 'No' you might want to reconsider your choice of field. Archaeology is an extremely rigorous and competitive profession.

Training

To qualify as a professional archaeologist, graduate study leading to a master's degree is necessary. A doctoral degree is often preferable. Most graduate programs in archaeology are found in anthropology departments. There are about thirty or so universities maintaining schools of archaeology; these can be found in *Peterson's Guide to Graduate and Professional Programs*. To gain the necessary background on the undergraduate level, a study of anthropology, history, art, geology, or a related field should be pursued. At the graduate level, students following a course in archaeology would also have to include cultural and physical anthropology and linguistics in their curricula.

Job Outlook

Relatively few openings exist in the field of teaching archaeology. Recently, however, more federal grants and contracts have been made available for archaeological fieldwork and research. A lot of this work is being conducted in the western and southwestern states, such as Colorado, Arizona, and New Mexico. Particularly in northwestern New Mexico, there is a strong industry developing resources such as gas and oil. Because much of the land there is owned by the Bureau of Land Management, the developers have to hire professional archaeologists to clear the site before gas lines or wells can be put in.

In addition to that, the building of a reservoir on the Dolores River in Colorado uncovered hundreds of archaeological sites, necessitating a great deal of archaeological work. The project, which is the largest on the continent, with a very attractive budget, has since brought many archaeologists to that area.

Interested scholars who do not desire a full-time professional career as an archaeologist but would like to experience archaeological work can find many opportunities to try their hands at a dig. If you are willing to invest your time and, in some cases, your money, you can easily find professionally supervised archaeological investigations taking on volunteers. These are listed in *Archaeology* magazine or in the books mentioned at the end of this chapter.

Center for American Archeology
Department B
Kampsville Archeological Center
P.O. Box 366
Kampsville, IL 62053

Crow Canyon Archaeological Center
23390 County Road K
Cortez, CO 81321

Earthwatch
680 Mount Auburn Street
Box 403N
Watertown, MA 02272

Foundations for Field Research
P.O. Box 2010
Alpine, CA 91001

The Smithsonian Institution
Smithsonian National Associates
Research Expedition Program
490 L'Enfant Plaza SW, Suite 4210
Washington, DC 20560

University Research Expeditions Program
Department J-4
University of California
Berkeley, CA 94720

Crow Canyon Archaeological Center

Crow Canyon is a nonprofit research and educational institution funded by tuition fees, donations, and federal grants. They have an eighty-acre campus in southwestern Colorado, near Mesa Verde National Park, with a staff of fifty or so archaeologists, educators, and support staff. In addition to their own research, they instruct participants, both adults and children, who want to learn about archaeology. From junior high age on, participants are taken into the field and taught excavation, recording, and documentation techniques. They also work in the lab a few days a week learning analysis techniques and methods for cleaning artifacts.

Children too young to work in the field can still participate in a simulated dig in a lab Crow Canyon has set up for that purpose. There they can learn the same excavating techniques as they sift through large shallow sand boxes where artifacts and walls and other features are buried, just as they would be in the field.

Participants come from all over the United States on educational vacations and stay for a three- to five-day program. Crow Canyon also works with about a dozen graduate students of archaeology a year, providing rewarding internships.

During the summer months, participants sleep in cabin tents or hogans, circular Navajo-style structures.

In Montezuma County, where Crow Canyon is located, there are more than ten thousand archaeological sites. Crow Canyon professionals are working at two different nearby sites—Sand Canyon Pueblo and Castle Rock Pueblo, both on Bureau of Land Management land. The sites were once Anasazi Indian villages. The Anasazi are the ancestors of present-day Pueblo Indians and were in this area of Colorado from the sixth century until about the year 1300. When they vacated the area, they headed for various points south and relocated. The Crow Canyon team's research is focusing on when exactly the Anasazi left and why.

They are also investigating the political and social systems of the Anasazi.

What It's Really Like

Kristin Kuckelman, Field Archaeologist

Kristin Kuckelman is a field archaeologist at Crow Canyon Archaeological Center. Her interest began when she was a child. Kristin's father was in the U.S. Air Force, and she traveled with her parents around the world. They were interested in different cultures and in archaeology as well and passed that interest on to their daughter. When it came time to go to college, Kristin was drawn to the anthropology program.

"I love the variety of it, I enjoy working outdoors, I enjoy writing," Kristin explains about her job. "And with any kind of research, there's the excitement of discovery. You're trying to solve problems, you're trying to find things out, you're trying to learn something new. And, basically, every time you go in the field, you hope you're going to learn something about a culture that no one knew before. You don't know what that's going to be; you never really know how it's going to turn out or what you're going to find.

"The sites in this particular area are very easy to discern. They have many hundreds of masonry rooms with, even after centuries, telltale piles of rubble and thousands of artifacts scattered about the ground. Just from walking around the modern ground surface you can see the tops of the walls and the depressions in the ground indicating the subterranean chambers.

"Sand Canyon covers about four acres; Castle Rock is smaller, close to three acres, and is situated around the base of a butte, a small flat-topped mountain.

"Because of the subterranean chambers, we sometimes have to dig down to two and a half to three meters to find the actual floor of the structure. The surface rooms are shallower, but we can still have a meter or a meter and a half filled in.

"We've found lithic artifacts, which are artifacts made out of stone, such as spear and arrow points, and sandstone tools for grinding grain. We've also found tens of thousands of pottery fragments—very rarely do we find a piece that is still intact. And very rarely do we engage in refitting, trying to piece the shards together. With so many pieces scattered over the ground, it would take many years, would be very, very expensive, and would certainly drive someone crazy!

"Beginning with the first week in May, which is the start of our field season, my partner and I head out to the site, set up equipment, and make sure we have the areas we want excavated all laid out and prepared. We take care of all our paperwork and any mapping we have to do so we're ready for participants to begin digging. During the digging season, we take participants out two or three days a week, but the first full day is spent on campus. Our educators give them a full orientation about archaeology in general. Out in the field, we give them a site tour to give them a background on what it is we're going to be digging, why we're digging, what we're trying to learn. We then give them tools and individual instruction and place them, either individually or in pairs, at the particular places we want excavated.

"Basically we move dirt and put it in a bucket and then take it to a screening station, which is a quarter-inch mesh screen. The dirt gets sifted through the screen to make sure we're not losing any artifacts. Everybody has his or her own bag to keep artifacts from each excavation area separate.

"Near the end of the season, we have quite a bit of documentation and mapping to do, and we wash and analyze the artifacts. When we're finished with them, most of the artifacts are put in storage, though a few are rotated as exhibits at the Anasazi Heritage Center, a federally run curation facility.

"Then we have to fill the areas we've dug back in with all the screened dirt and rocks we originally dug out. The idea is if you were to walk across the site a year later, you'd never know there had been an excavation there. For safety reasons, we can't leave gaping holes in the land, and, in terms of conservation, to leave a pit open to the elements would damage the site. Before we close it back up, we line the pit with landscaping fabric to protect it and to provide a clue in case future archaeologists are digging there but do not have access to our notes and maps. The lining would show them the site had already been excavated. There are so many sites, and to keep a site open and developed for public exhibit, as has been done at Mesa Verde, would be extremely expensive. It would also be very hard on the architecture itself. Constant maintenance would have to be performed, or everything would eventually deteriorate.

"During the winter we write up in report form everything we learned the previous summer. We also write articles for professional journals and present papers at archaeological conferences across the country."

Kristin Kuckelman's Background

Kristin graduated in 1975 with a bachelor's degree in anthropology and psychology from Colorado Women's College (which has now merged with the University of Denver) and earned her master's degree in anthropology with a concentration in archaeology from the University of Texas at Austin in 1977.

Further Reading

Books and Guides

The Adventure of Archeology, by Brian M. Fagan, National Geographic Society, Washington, D.C.

America's Ancient Treasures, by Franklin and Mary Elting,
    University of New Mexico Press.
Archaeological Fieldwork Opportunities Bulletin, compiled by
    the Archaeological Institute of America, can be ordered
    through Kendall Hunt Publishing Company, Order
    Department, 2640 Kerper Boulevard, Dubuque, IA 52001. It
    is a comprehensive guide to excavations, field schools, and
    special programs throughout the world with openings for
    volunteers, students, staff, and technicians.
Archaeology: Theories, Methods, and Practice, by Colin
    Renfrew and Paul Bahn, Thames and Hudson, New York.
*Directory of Historical Organizations in the United States and
    Canada*, by the American Association for State and Local
    History. More than thirteen thousand listings of historical
    and genealogical societies, museums, archives, and other
    history-related groups.
LEAP: Listing of Education in Archeological Programs,
    available from: LEAP Coordinator, DCA/ADD, National
    Park Service, P.O. Box 37127, Washington, DC 20013.
*Peterson's Guide to Graduate and Professional Programs: An
    Overview*, Peterson's Guides, Princeton, N.J.
Summer Field School List, American Anthropological
    Association, 1703 New Hampshire Avenue NW,
    Washington, DC 20009.

Magazines

Archaeology, bimonthly published by the Archaeological
    Institute of America
National Geographic, monthly
Scientific American, monthly
Smithsonian, monthly

Professional Journals

These journals, though not available in every local library, can be found in university libraries or in large public libraries.

American Antiquity
Historical Archaeology
Journal of Anthropological Archaeology
Journal of Field Archaeology
North American Archaeologist

CHAPTER SIX

Psychologists

W hile some psychologists are clinicians, working in a therapeutic relationship with patients or clients, others study human behavior and mental processes to understand, explain, and change people's behavior. They may study the way a person thinks, feels, or behaves. Research psychologists investigate the physical, cognitive, emotional, or social aspects of human behavior. Like other social scientists, psychologists formulate hypotheses and collect data to test their validity. Research methods depend on the topic under study. Psychologists may gather information through controlled laboratory experiments; personality, performance, aptitude, and intelligence tests; observation, interviews, and questionnaires; clinical studies; or surveys. Computers are widely used to record and analyze this information.

Psychologists in applied fields counsel and conduct training programs; do market research; apply psychological treatments to a variety of medical and surgical conditions; or provide mental health services in hospitals, clinics, or private settings.

Because psychology deals with human behavior, psychologists apply their knowledge and techniques to a wide range of endeavors, including human services, management, education, law, and sports. In addition to the variety of work settings, psychologists specialize in many different areas.

Clinical psychologists, who constitute the largest specialty, generally work in independent or group practice or in hospitals or clinics. They may help the mentally or emotionally disturbed adjust to life and are increasingly helping all kinds of medical and surgical patients deal with their illnesses or injuries. They may work in physical medicine and rehabilitation settings, treating patients with spinal cord injuries, chronic pain or illness, stroke, and arthritis and neurologic conditions, such as multiple sclerosis. Others help people deal with life stresses such as divorce or aging.

Clinical psychologists interview patients; give diagnostic tests; provide individual, family, and group psychotherapy; and design and implement behavior modification programs. They may collaborate with physicians and other specialists in developing treatment programs and help patients understand and comply with the prescribed treatment. Some clinical psychologists work in universities, where they train graduate students in the delivery of mental health and behavioral medicine services. Others administer community mental health programs.

Counseling psychologists perform many of the same functions as clinical psychologists and use several techniques, including interviewing and testing, to advise people on how to deal with problems of everyday living—personal, social, educational, or vocational.

Developmental psychologists study the patterns and causes of behavioral change as people progress through life from infancy to adulthood. Some concern themselves with behavior during infancy, childhood, and adolescence, while others study changes that take place during maturity and old age. The study of developmental disabilities and how they affect a person and others is a new area within developmental psychology.

Educational psychologists evaluate student and teacher needs and design and develop programs to enhance the educational setting.

Experimental psychologists study behavior processes and work with human beings and animals, such as rats, monkeys, and pigeons. Prominent areas of experimental research include motivation, thinking, attention, learning and retention, sensory and perceptual processes, effects of substance use and abuse, and genetic and neurological factors in behavior.

Industrial and organizational psychologists apply psychological techniques to personnel administration, management, and marketing problems. They are involved in policy planning, applicant screening, training and development, psychological test research, counseling, and organizational development and analysis. For example, an industrial psychologist may work with management to develop better training programs and to reorganize the work setting to improve worker productivity or quality of work life.

School psychologists work with students, teachers, parents, and administrators to resolve students' learning and behavior problems.

Social psychologists examine people's interactions with others and with the social environment. Prominent areas of study include group behavior, leadership, attitudes, and interpersonal perception.

The following are some relatively new specialties:

Cognitive psychologists deal with the brain's role in memory, thinking, and perceptions; some are involved with research related to computer programming and artificial intelligence.

Health psychologists promote good health through health maintenance counseling programs that are designed, for example, to help people stop smoking or lose weight.

Neuropsychologists study the relation between the brain and behavior. They often work in stroke and head injury programs.

Geropsychologists deal with the special problems faced by the elderly. The emergence and growth of these specialties reflects the increasing participation of psychologists in providing direct services to special patient populations.

Other areas of specialization include psychometrics, history of psychology, psychology and the arts, psychopharmacology, and community, comparative, consumer, engineering, environmental, family, forensic, population, military, and rehabilitation psychology. Many people also hold positions as psychology faculty at colleges and universities and as high school psychology teachers.

A psychologist's specialty and place of employment determine working conditions. For example, clinical, school, and counseling psychologists in private practice have pleasant, comfortable offices and set their own hours. However, they often have evening hours to accommodate their clients.

Some employed in hospitals, nursing homes, and other health facilities often work evenings and weekends, while others in schools and clinics work regular hours.

Psychologists employed by academic institutions divide their hours among teaching, research, and administrative responsibilities. Some maintain part-time consulting practices as well.

In contrast to the many psychologists who have flexible work schedules, most in government and private industry have more structured schedules. Reading and writing research reports, they often work alone. Many experience the pressures of deadlines, tight schedules, and overtime work. Their routines may be interrupted frequently. Travel may be required to attend conferences or conduct research.

After several years of experience, some psychologists, usually those with doctoral degrees, enter private practice or set up their own research or consulting firms. A growing proportion of psychologists are self-employed.

Job Outlook

Psychologists held about 144,000 jobs in 1994. Educational institutions employed nearly four out of ten salaried psychologists in positions involving counseling, testing, special education, research, and administration; hospitals, mental health clinics, rehabilitation centers, nursing homes, and other health facilities employed three out of ten; and government agencies at the federal, state, and local levels employed one-sixth. The Department of Veterans Affairs, the Department of Defense, and the Public

Health Service employ the overwhelming majority of psychologists working for federal agencies. Governments employ psychologists in hospitals, clinics, correctional facilities, and other settings. Psychologists also work in social service organizations, research organizations, management consulting firms, marketing research firms, and other businesses.

Employment of psychologists is expected to grow faster than the average for all occupations through the year 2005. Largely because of the substantial investment in training required to enter this specialized field, psychologists have a strong attachment to the occupation; only a small proportion leave the profession each year. Nevertheless, replacement needs are expected to account for most job openings, similar to most occupations.

Programs to combat the increase in alcohol abuse, drug dependency, marital strife, family violence, crime, and other problems plaguing society should stimulate employment growth. Other factors spurring demand for psychologists include increased emphasis on mental health maintenance in conjunction with the treatment of physical illness; public concern for the development of human resources, including the growing elderly population; increased testing and counseling of children; and more interest in rehabilitation of prisoners. Changes in the level of government funding for these kinds of services could affect the demand for psychologists.

Job opportunities in health care should remain strong, particularly in health care provider networks, such as health maintenance and preferred provider organizations, that specialize in mental health and in nursing homes and alcohol and drug abuse rehabilitation programs. Job opportunities will arise in businesses, nonprofit organizations, and research and computer firms. Companies will use the expertise of psychologists in survey design, analysis, and research to provide personnel testing, program evaluation, and statistical analysis. The increase in employee assistance programs in which psychologists help people stop smoking, control weight, or alter other behaviors also should spur job growth. The expected wave of retirements among college faculty, beginning in the late 1990s, should result in job openings for psychologists in colleges and universities.

Other openings are likely to occur as psychologists study the effectiveness of changes in health, education, military, law enforcement, and consumer protection programs. Psychologists also are increasingly studying the effects on people of technological advances in areas such as agriculture, energy, the conservation and use of natural resources, and industrial and office automation.

Opportunities are best for candidates with doctoral degrees. Persons holding doctorates from leading universities in applied areas such as school, clinical, counseling, health, industrial, and educational psychology should have particularly good prospects.

Psychologists with extensive training in quantitative research methods and computer science may have a competitive edge over applicants without this background.

Graduates with master's degrees in psychology may encounter competition for the limited number of jobs for which they qualify. Those with master's degrees in school psychology should have the best job prospects, as schools are expected to increase student counseling and mental health services. Some master's degree holders may find jobs as psychological assistants in community mental health centers—these positions often require direct supervision by a licensed psychologist.

Others may find jobs involving research, data collection, and analysis in universities, government, or private companies.

Bachelor's degree holders can expect very few opportunities directly related to psychology. Some may find jobs as assistants in rehabilitation centers or in other jobs involving data collection and analysis.

Those who meet state certification requirements may become high school psychology teachers.

Training

A doctoral degree generally is required for employment as a psychologist. Psychologists with doctorates qualify for a wide range of teaching, research, clinical, and counseling positions in universities, elementary and secondary schools, private industry, and government.

Psychologists who have earned the doctor of psychology (Psy.D.) qualify mainly for clinical positions. Those with master's degrees in psychology can administer tests as psychological assistants. Under the supervision of doctoral-level psychologists, they can conduct research in laboratories, perform psychological evaluations, counsel patients, or perform administrative duties. They may teach in high schools or two-year colleges or work as school psychologists or counselors.

A bachelor's degree in psychology qualifies a person to assist psychologists and other professionals in community mental health centers, vocational rehabilitation offices, and correctional programs; to work as a research or administrative assistant; and to take a jobs as a trainee in government or business. However, without additional academic training, advancement opportunities in psychology are severely limited.

In the federal government, candidates having at least twenty-four semester hours in psychology and one course in statistics qualify for entry-level positions. Competition for these jobs is keen, however. Clinical psychologists generally must have completed the Ph.D. or Psy.D. requirements and have served an internship; vocational and guidance counselors usually need two years of graduate study in counseling and one year of counseling experience.

In most cases, two years of full-time graduate study are needed to earn a master's degree in psychology. Requirements include practical experience in an applied setting or a thesis based on a research project. A master's in school psychology requires about two years of course work and a one-year internship.

Five to seven years of graduate work usually are required for a doctoral degree. The Ph.D. degree culminates in a dissertation based on original research. Courses in quantitative research methods, which include the use of computers, are an integral part of graduate study and usually are necessary to complete the dissertation.

The Psy.D. usually is based on practical work and examinations rather than a dissertation. In clinical or counseling psychology, the requirements for the doctoral degree generally include a year or more of internship or supervised experience.

Competition for admission into most graduate programs is keen. Some universities require an undergraduate major in psychology. Others prefer only basic psychology with courses in the biological, physical, and social sciences, statistics, and mathematics.

Most colleges and universities offer a bachelor's degree program in psychology; several hundred offer a master's and/or a Ph.D. program. A relatively small number of professional schools of psychology, some affiliated with colleges or universities, offer the Psy.D.

The American Psychological Association (APA) presently accredits doctoral training programs in clinical, counseling, and school psychology. The National Council for Accreditation of Teacher Education, with the assistance of the National Association of School Psychologists, also is involved in the accreditation of advanced degree programs in school psychology. The APA also accredits institutions that provide internships for doctoral students in school, clinical, and counseling psychology.

Although financial aid is difficult to obtain, some universities award fellowships or scholarships or arrange for part-time employment. The Veterans Administration (VA) offers predoctoral traineeships to interns in VA hospitals, clinics, and related training agencies. The National Science Foundation, the Department of Health and Human Services, and many other organizations also provide grants to psychology departments to help fund student stipends.

Psychologists in independent practice or those who offer any type of patient care, including clinical, counseling, and school psychologists, must meet certification or licensing requirements. All states and the District of Columbia have such requirements.

Licensing laws vary by state but generally require a doctorate in psychology, completion of an approved internship, and one to two years of professional experience. In addition, most states require that applicants pass an examination. Most state boards administer a standardized test and, in many instances, additional oral or essay examinations. Very few states certify those with a master's degree as psychological assistants or associates. Some states require continuing education for license renewal.

Most states require that licensed or certified psychologists limit their practices to those areas in which they have developed professional competence through training and experience.

The American Board of Professional Psychology recognizes professional achievement by awarding diplomas primarily in clinical psychology, clinical neuropsychology, and counseling, forensic, industrial and organizational, and school psychology. Candidates need a doctorate in psychology, five years of experience, and professional endorsements; they also must pass an examination.

Even more so than in other occupations, aspiring psychologists who are interested in direct patient care must be emotionally stable, mature, and able to deal effectively with people. Sensitivity, compassion, and the ability to lead and inspire others are particularly important for clinical work and counseling.

Research psychologists should be able to work independently and as part of a team. Verbal and writing skills are necessary to communicate treatment and research findings. Patience and perseverance are vital qualities because results from psychological treatment of patients or research often are long in coming.

Salaries

According to a 1993 survey by the American Psychological Association, the median annual salary of psychologists with a doctoral degree was $39,100 in counseling psychology; $39,000 in research positions; $40,000 in clinical psychology; and $45,000 in school psychology. From an earlier survey, median annual salaries in industrial/organizational psychology were $76,000; in university psychology departments, median annual salaries ranged from $32,000 for assistant professors to $55,000 for full professors.

The median annual salary of master's degree holders was $35,000 for faculty; $26,000 in counseling psychology; $24,000 in clinical psychology; $28,000 in research positions; $58,000 in industrial/organizational psychology; and $34,500 in school psychology. Some psychologists have much higher earnings, particularly those in private practice.

The federal government recognizes education and experience in certifying applicants for entry-level positions. In general, the average starting salary for psychologists having a bachelor's degree was about $18,700 a year in 1995; those with superior academic records could begin at $23,200. Counseling and school psychologists with a master's degree and one year of counseling experience could start at $28,300. Clinical psychologists having a Ph.D. or Psy.D. degree and one year of internship could start at $34,300; some individuals could start at $41,100.

The average salary for psychologists in the federal government in nonsupervisory, supervisory, and managerial positions was about $58,300 a year in 1995.

What It's Really Like

Denise Stybr, School Psychologist

Denise Stybr has been a school psychologist with the Center Cass School District #66 in Downers Grove, Illinois, since 1990. In 1979 she earned a bachelor of science degree in psychology from the University of Illinois, Urbana. Her master of arts degree in school psychology is from Governors State University in Illinois. She began her professional career in 1982.

"I administer psychoeducational testing to determine the presence or absence of a disabling condition, such as a learning disability, mental retardation, or emotional disorder," Denise Stybr explains. "I also provide individual and group counseling to the students, consultation to the parents and staff, and design behavior management programs.

"My job is extremely stressful but never boring. I make life-changing decisions that affect both children and their families. From the moment I get to work, generally 7:30 A.M., until the moment I leave, generally 4:30 P.M., I am on. I am often met in the parking lot with questions and concerns. It is common for me to work the whole day with only a half an hour break at lunch. A typical day finds me attending several meetings at which we are usually deciding if a child should be tested and if he qualifies for services after the tests have been completed. Or I'm presenting the test results to his parents.

"In between meetings, I usually hold two to three counseling sessions, spend two to three hours testing and the remainder of the time writing reports, talking to teachers, or talking to parents. I travel to three schools, often on the same day. The office space I'm allocated ranges from very nice to nonexistent.

"I do not like the stress level or, all too often, feeling that no matter what I do it isn't going to be enough for this child. But I do like the freedom and variety of my job. I rarely have to do any one thing at a specific time (with the exception of meetings). I can choose when to do what. I have control over my time."

Denise Stybr's Background

"I originally had thought to become a psychiatrist but decided that medical school was not for me by my junior year in college. I then researched the different areas of graduate study for psychology and liked the freedom of school psychology. I do not have to maintain my own office or records. I do not have to purchase malpractice insurance for myself. I do not have to get coverage to go on a vacation. I never have to turn someone down who needs help but can't pay. (It's a free service through the schools.) And I mainly work with children ages three to fourteen. In this age range, lots of progress is still relatively easy to make.

"In order to practice as a certified school psychologist you must also complete a one school-year internship, during which time you act as a school psychologist but are closely supervised by a certified school psychologist. In addition, seventy-five contact hours of continuing educational activities must be completed and documented every three years in order to continue to be nationally certificated.

"The reason I have a B.S. instead of a B.A. is that I originally was intent on medical school, so I took more science courses than required for a B.A. My M.S. is a special kind of master's degree. In fact, it is often called a 'specialist degree' because it requires fifty-seven or more hours versus a regular master's that usually requires thirty to thirty-two hours."

Some Advice from Denise Stybr

"Being a school psychologist requires a certain personality type, almost more than it does any special talent. One must be structured and organized, yet flexible. One must know when to take a stand and when to back down. You have to have empathy, but not sympathy, and compassion without sentimentality. A school psychologist often works with no peer input and must remain impartial.

"Seek after-school and summer jobs that put you around children and their parents. If possible, volunteer with developmentally disabled children in order to see if you have what it takes to work with that population. Ask to observe in some special education classrooms.

"Don't expect to make a lot of money. School psychologists are often paid less than teachers. Benefits are often not as good as the teachers' contracts. Days are longer. We often work days during the summer that the teachers do not. Generally we work a week or two before school starts and after school ends. This is not an easy, high-paying job. It is truly a vocation more than an occupation."

Gerald D. Oster, Clinical Psychologist

Gerald D. Oster is a licensed psychologist with a private practice. He is also a clinical associate professor of psychiatry at the University of Maryland Medical School in Baltimore.

He earned his B.A. in sociology at the University of South Florida, Tampa, in 1971; his M.A. in psychology at Middle Tennessee State University in Murfreesboro in 1976; and his Ph.D. in psychology at Virginia Commonwealth University in Richmond in 1981.

"Since I have decided to have several jobs—and this was a conscious decision because I'm primarily a person who enjoys variety—my days also vary," he explains. "For instance, Tuesday mornings find me for two hours at a community mental health center in the inner city of Baltimore, where I work as a child and family therapist. Right now I'm working with two particular patients. One is a sixteen-year-old youth who had trouble with the law. He served time in juvenile delinquent centers and now is trying to make it back into the community but is struggling to fit in at school and in his foster care placement.

"The other is a child in kindergarten who is very insecure about the world around him. He lives in a very dangerous neighborhood with his grandparents as his primary caretakers. His mother, who also lives with him, is a drug addict.

"When I am not seeing these two patients, I am doing the enormous paperwork required by the various governing agencies that monitor the clinic.

"After catching up at the clinic (I work at home and in my private practice on Mondays), I spend an eight-hour period at the University Counseling Center, where I see the opposite of the spectrum—very intelligent and creative individuals who are in various professional schools (law, medicine, social work, and so forth). Although quite articulate and resourceful, they, too, have their own struggles and often make good use of the support that our center provides. Usually, they come to us due to the stress of school but also due to life's complications, meaning problems in relationships, caretaking of others (many are married or have relatives or children that they are responsible for). Also, the pace and expectations for learning are incredible and require a huge sacrifice socially that many have a difficult time adjusting to. After these hours are over, I usually go to my private practice to sort through the mail or see an occasional evening patient.

"My other days are similar but involve different demands and different populations each day. Sometimes I am at the local community hospital interviewing or testing a suicidal or out-of-control adolescent. My private practice is divided between seeing children and adults with an assortment of problems that might stem from family discord, learning difficulties in school and their emotional impact, and relationship problems (of which there are many variations).

"I stay quite busy but always have to seek out new ways to maintain my practice, especially in the context of managed care. For myself and many of my colleagues in a solo private practice, this has become a nightmare with entangled paperwork and never being sure of payment. This has made life more problematic and anxiety provoking. This has also affected the hospitals where I work and has created uncertainty in many of the health professions. The future depends on adapting to these changes and using different skills to negotiate new expectations."

Gerald Oster's Background

"My undergraduate experience, from 1967 to 1971, was a time of social change and activism—and self-exploration. Although I began as a business major, the courses in sociology were much more appealing, and the people's thinking in those courses were more similar to my viewpoints at the time.

"The prospect of studying topics such as social and political theory and how people adapt to environmental and economic change was very appealing. And the prospect of studying these topics on a higher level was challenging. I was taking school and studying seriously, both on an undergraduate and graduate level.

"Also, learning about and helping people in all aspects of life filled a need in myself to go beyond my own boundaries and provide support to people in stress or to help the broader institutions in gaining the appropriate placement for people who needed assistance, whether it was the aged, juvenile delinquents, or children with learning problems.

"It was not until several years after receiving my undergraduate degree (and owning a bookstore for several years) that I was able to crystallize my thoughts into a single direction. I am sure this waiting is not unique. Only a few have a specific direction regarding careers, and most go through college with the hope that the degree and higher education will get them some kind of a job. However, a career choice means much more. It is something that you know that you love and want to pursue full-time; in essence, it becomes a paid hobby.

"For me, psychology was that path. And even in psychology, there were many roads to pursue. At first, I wanted to be a criminal psychologist and found courses in personality and psychopathology very fascinating. I also found courses in child development extremely interesting and had an outstanding professor that was able to demonstrate the early cognitive and emotional stages of life. My first choice, criminal psychology, took me to my first graduate school and my master's degree and actually work within the juvenile justice system, providing evaluations for the courts on delinquents. However, through the support of my professors and continuing interest in all of psychology, I applied and was able to get into a doctoral program where I was exposed to a greater depth and breadth of psychology.

"While there, I worked in a rat laboratory, was part of a developing center for aging, taught courses in developmental psychology and child development, and was exposed to continuing clinical work through practicums at child development centers and psychiatric units for the aged. I also participated with many research teams on topics of learning theory, intellectual testing, and cognitive changes over the life span.

"I started my professional career in 1981 at a private research firm that subcontracted work from the National Institutes of Health (NIH). At the time, I was involved coordinating research projects for a nationwide study on depression. After a year, I decided to return to clinical work and obtained a job in a state hospital as a psychologist on an adolescent unit. During that time, I also consulted to a geriatric unit and continued my learning through weekly seminars and clinical rounds.

"After several years and having obtained my independent professional license, I changed locations and jobs. I began working at a residential treatment center for emotionally disturbed children and adolescents. While there I became director of psychology internship training. I also continued my own training, which included study in family therapy at a well-known institute. I then became interested in expanding my private practice and continuing my writing, which I had begun during this time. So, I resigned and began collecting a series of part-time jobs.

"As far as my writing, I have now coauthored six professional books on psychological testing and therapy. I have also cowritten a trade book, titled *Helping Your Depressed Teenager: A Guide for Parents and Caregivers* (Wiley, 1995). My latest book is *Clinical Uses of Drawings* (Jason Aronson, 1996)."

Some Advice from Gerald Oster

"Learning is a lifelong process. Degrees only give you permission to learn. These were words from an uncle and ring true in today's world. Most people anticipate change, and you can expect to change career paths several times during a lifetime. Thus, going to college and possibly to graduate school allows you this exposure to not only the gathering of technical skills but also to possibilities. Even a field such as psychology has numerous outlets to pursue. In research, there is test development, treatment outcomes, human factors studies, to name a few. In clinical psychology, you can work in hospitals, outpatient centers, residential treatment, and with various populations, such as infants, parent training, teenagers, adults with serious mental illness, or support to the healthy aged. Organizational psychologists work in office settings to devise screening tests, support the emotional needs of the staff, or do staff development seminars. And psychologists teach courses in developmental or social issues, learning theory or cognitive-behavioral therapy; one of my friends even teaches 'psychology of peach' studies.

"Along the way, you can define yourself in many ways. What it takes is sticking to a broad path and having the realization that the path may have many branches that are all quite good. But it takes exposure to these branches to realize the possibilities. So look around, read articles from journals or magazines by people who are doing the kind of work you can see yourself doing. And find out what is exciting and meaningful to you. Don't be afraid to talk to these people (they are human and approachable). If not them, talk to your professors; they want to help and have placed themselves as models and as valuable resources.

"Gain experience wherever you can, through paid or volunteer work. Go to seminars and to conventions, even if these are supposed to be for professionals. There is no better place to see the kinds of possibilities than at a national convention within a profession. You gain incredible exposure and an awareness of what the field is all about. Discovering your life's pursuit, something that you really love, is especially important, especially in the context of family.

"Also, gain mentors along the way. Become an assistant, whether it is in teaching or research. This is an excellent way to discover what your strengths and weaknesses are and whether you could see yourself doing this work on a daily basis. Take as many practicums or internships as possible.

"And travel. In striving for an ideal picture of yourself, you also want to be aware of possible settings. Do you enjoy the outdoors or city life? Does your profession offer more possibilities in small towns, where you actually perform more duties, than in large cities, where there are many specialists but more people, job opportunities, and so on. What type of atmosphere do you prefer—the pressure of the Northeast or the slower pace of the South or the alternative lifestyles of the Southwest?"

CHAPTER SEVEN

Museum Curators

*I*f you ask some people what they think of museums, they might tell you that the word itself conjures up images of yawn-stifling tours of quiet, tomblike places, the atmosphere as inspiring as the inside of a crypt. The idea of displaying and examining the art and artifacts that make up the world's history reminds them of dry school lessons filled with impossible-to-remember names and dates and events that no longer hold any meaning for life today.

Fortunately, that perception is not as widely shared as those uninitiated would like you to believe. But if you are reading this book, you already know that. Museums are not dull and lifeless structures displaying dull and lifeless artifacts. They are as exciting as a space launch or a Civil War battlefield, an African safari or a Roman amphitheater.

Patrons of the arts, history lovers, and those who also look to the future have continuously provided enthusiastic support to museums, ensuring their survival through the ages. From meager beginnings, thousands of museums now flourish throughout the world, displaying a wide range of collections.

Museums are no longer repositories for just art or ancient relics. They house everything from moon rocks to the ruby slippers Judy Garland wore in the *Wizard of Oz*. And as varied as the collections are, so are the opportunities for employment. In this chapter we will explore the different kinds of museums and the career paths they offer.

Today, there are as many different kinds of museums as the items they display or the topics they explain. Some are famous establishments, such as those that comprise the Smithsonian Institution; others are small enterprises, known only locally.

The Different Kinds of Museums

Art Museums

Art museums are where objects of aesthetic value are preserved and displayed. Art museums have a variety of functions, including acquiring, conserving, and exhibiting works of art; providing art education for the general public; and conducting art historical research.

History Museums

From acquiring collections and preserving them to explaining and displaying them, in history museums dedicated professionals have the chance to work with every aspect of the relics and other forms of physical evidence of the past. History museums can cover a particular period, such as Colonial America, or a particular topic, such as entertainment or advertising.

A history museum's collection could be displayed in a modern building constructed specifically for that purpose, or the building itself, along with its contents, could be the museum. Examples include the homes of famous people such as Paul Revere or Thomas Jefferson or historic structures such as lighthouses or old courthouses.

Living History Museums

A living history museum is a vibrant, active village, town, or city where the day-to-day life of a particular time period has been authentically recreated. The houses and public buildings are restored originals or thoroughly researched reproductions. Interiors are outfitted with period furniture, cookware, bed linens, and tablecloths.

Employees known as character interpreters function as residents, wearing the clothing of the day and discussing their dreams and concerns with visitors as they go about their daily tasks. They often must research the lives of the characters they portray as well as the customs of the time period.

Colonial Williamsburg in Virginia and Plimoth Plantation in Massachusetts are just two examples of living history museums.

Natural History Museums

Natural history museums are dedicated to research, exhibition, and education in the natural sciences. Museums vary in size and collections and could include all or some of the following departments: anthropology, astronomy, botany, entomology, fossil and living vertebrates, geology, herpetology and ichthyology, mammalogy, mineralogy, ornithology, and vertebrate paleontology.

Collections could include artifacts from ancient civilizations, gems and jewels, fossils, meteorites, and animals from around the world displayed in lifelike settings.

Science Museums and Discovery Centers

Science museums preserve and display objects that have been important to the development of science and technology. Science centers or discovery centers, as they are sometimes called, generally teach the principles related to these fields. They often involve visitors in hands-on activities, many catering particularly to children. The two types of science museums are not necessarily mutually exclusive, although most institutions fall into one category or the other.

Planetariums

Planetariums are structures, usually with dome ceilings, that are outfitted to give audiences the illusion of being outside under a starlit sky. Through the use of projectors, slides, movies, and computers, the location of the planets and stars and all sorts of astronomical activity can be demonstrated.

Planetariums are often part of a science museum complex, with most large cities now having full-scale facilities. They are used as tourist and educational attractions with elaborate space exhibits or public observational facilities. Smaller planetariums are also associated with universities and are used for classroom instruction in geography, navigation, and astronomy.

Jobs Within Museums

Professional job classifications within museums can fall into several categories, including administration, collections, curation, education and interpretation, development (fund-raising), exhibit design, and research.

Many job titles are common to each kind of museum, but the job description will vary depending on the institution. Curators, exhibit designers, and researchers, for example, are found in almost every kind of museum, from art to science and history museums, even though the collections they deal with and their specific duties are very different.

In this chapter you will be introduced to a curator at the Smithsonian and a researcher at Plimoth Plantation.

Curator

Curators are specialists in a particular academic discipline relevant to a museum's collections. They are generally responsible for the care and interpretation of all objects and specimens on loan or belonging to the museum, and they are fully knowledgeable about each object's history and importance.

Depending upon the museum and their own areas of interest, curators can work with textiles and costumes, paintings, memorabilia, historic structures, crafts, furniture, coins, or a variety of other historically significant items.

Education Requirements

A curator would normally possess an advanced degree with a concentration in an area related to the museum's collections.

Experience

Three years of experience in a museum or related educational or research facility would usually be required before a candidate could advance to a full curatorial position.

Knowledge and Skills

A curator must have the ability to explain and interpret the collection to the public and be familiar with the techniques of selection, evaluation, preservation, restoration, and exhibition of the museum's collection.

The Ideal Background

In addition to a job candidate's educational achievements, the American Association of Museums (AAM) suggests these qualifications for museum personnel:

"A museum professional should be expected to have a familiarity with the history, goals, and functions of museums; a knowledge of and commitment to the AAM statement on ethics; and a willingness to improve skills by study and by attendance at training sessions, seminars, and professional conferences.

"Dedication, integrity, diplomacy, and a commitment to thoroughness and accuracy are demanded of all museum professionals. The ability to communicate orally and in writing and to work constructively with associates is essential.

"An awareness of legal issues affecting museums and the ability to prepare and interpret budgets and grant applications are required of all positions. Additional knowledge, skills, and abilities, such as a second language, typing and word processing, and familiarity with the museum's community and its resources may be required for certain positions and are always beneficial and desirable."

What It's Really Like: Working at the National Museum of American History

The National Museum of American History, part of the Smithsonian Institution complex on the National Mall, is devoted to the exhibition, care, and study of artifacts that reflect the experience of the American people. The museum receives more than five million visitors a year. It has the responsibility for preserving more than sixteen million objects it has acquired over the last century, and it has more than 430 employees on staff.

Charles McGovern, Curator

Charles McGovern is supervisor of the American History Museum's division of community life, overseeing a group of technicians, specialists, collections-based researchers, curators, and support staff. He is also a curator, responsible for twentieth-century consumerism and popular culture. This department covers the history of entertainment, leisure, recreation, and commerce.

The exhibits within this department are probably the most popular and the most well known. Visitors to the museum come to view Judy Garland's ruby slippers from the *Wizard of Oz*, Archie Bunker's well-worn chair, or Edgar Bergen's famous wooden dummy, Charlie McCarthy.

Charles McGovern's interest in cultural history began at an early age. He watched a lot of television and listened to the radio and participated in the mass popular culture in the 1960s. His father and mother told him about the times when they were growing up, sharing with him stories about the early days of radio. When Charles got to high school and read books his teachers recommended, he realized that Babe Ruth and Laurel and Hardy and the Marx brothers, personalities he cared very deeply about, were as much a part of history as Calvin Coolidge or the first World War.

"Part of my profession as a historian is to be a decoder or an explainer," Charles McGovern explains, "to go back into the heads and the lives and the beliefs of our ancestors. And here, we try to do that respectfully, understanding the world as they saw it. As we do that, we see how culture reflects the times, the fears and ideals and problems of a given society. You cannot look at certain creations of our popular culture without seeing those kinds of elements in them.

"As a curator, I am responsible for the creation and maintenance of the collections in my subject area. I document the history of the everyday life of American people. The major outline for my job puts me in charge of building collections, developing exhibitions, conducting research, writing, public service, public speaking, and being a graduate advisor to eleven research fellows.

"Specifically, my job is divided into three parts: acquisitions (acquiring new objects and exhibits for the museum), exhibiting and interpreting, and research.

"The collections I am responsible for include a lot of the things related to the history of American entertainment: a hat that Jimmy Durante used in his stage appearances; Ann Miller's tap shoes; Howdy Doody; Mr. Moose, Bunny Rabbit, and the grandfather clock from 'Captain Kangaroo'; the suit of armor worn by Francis X. Bushman in the original 1936 movie *Ben Hur*; Carol Burnett's char lady costume; Mister Roger's sweater; Harrison Ford's Indiana Jones outfit—his leather jacket and hat; Tom Selleck's ring from 'Magnum, P.I.,' and his Hawaiian shirt and baseball cap; old 78 rpm records; movie posters; and comic books. We also look for collections that give us insight into

American consumerism and commerce. We have the bonnet that was worn by the woman who posed for the Sun-Maid Raisins box, a huge collection of turn-of-the-century advertising, marketing and packaging items from the Hills Brothers Coffee Company, and a collection of memorabilia from world fairs from 1851 to 1988.

"To build our collections we depend largely on people donating items. In fact, almost everything has been donated. We have very little money in our acquisitions budget. We can't compete in a very inflated market with the galleries and people who deal with 'collectibles.' People must be willing to donate, so we look for people who either don't need the money or get the point of what we're trying to do.

"Sometimes we're not able to accept everything that is being offered. Someone called once and wanted to donate Charlie Chaplin's cane. But first, how do I know that it was his cane— it's impossible to document that. And second, Chaplin probably went through thousands of canes. Those bamboo things snapped very easily. Something like that we couldn't take.

"And although I must be familiar with every piece's history, the range and variety of items I am responsible for is staggering. It's not as if I were a curator of painting where I'm trained in oils and brush techniques. Once in a while I have to confer with an appraiser or dealer to determine authenticity.

"Once a donation has been accepted, we can never promise that it will go on display. Less than 2 percent of our collection is on display at any given time; the rest is kept in storage. Although some exhibits, such as the ruby slippers or Archie's chair, are permanent, others rotate.

"Part of my job is to decide what gets exhibited, what gets stored, what is rotated. And to care for all the items, to make sure they don't deteriorate, we need to remove even permanent exhibits from time to time. People travel a long way expecting to see a certain item, and if it's not on display they're usually upset. They don't realize they should check with us first if they're coming to see something in particular. We took Charlie McCarthy off to clean him one day, and within a half an hour we had three phone calls asking where was Charlie McCarthy.

"The exhibiting side of my job is really a team effort. Exhibit designers work with curators to decide *how* an item should be displayed. The designer is responsible for the layout of objects and text and graphics and props. A conservator, someone who takes care of the actual repair or maintenance of an object, would be responsible for the 'prescription'—'this piece needs to be lit with no more than thirty-foot candles,' for example.

"But I feel that research is really my first duty. All the collecting and exhibiting doesn't mean anything unless you have something to say. You have to figure out first what point you're making. Our point is the showing of everyday life of the American people, and for earlier times that's something that has to be researched. Of course, you do research to support the things you already have in your collection, but the research also helps you to determine what you should be out there collecting."

Charles McGovern's Background

Charles studied at Swarthmore College in Pennsylvania and finished in 1980 with a B.A. with honors in history. He immediately began graduate school at Harvard and earned his A.M. in history in 1983 and his Ph.D. in American civilization in 1993.

Charles taught history at Harvard, then from 1986 through 1987, he was at the Smithsonian as a research fellow. In 1988 he returned to the Smithsonian as a full-time curator.

The Smithsonian as a Training Ground

Every year, the Smithsonian awards dozens of research fellowships, providing funding to doctoral candidates and access to museum collections. To be hired as curators, candidates must have earned or nearly completed their doctorates. Entry-level positions include technicians and specialists and research-related jobs. Paid internships and volunteer positions are usually available and are a good way to get a foot in the door.

Charles McGovern points out that jobs for curators at the Smithsonian seldom become available. But because the Smithsonian has a certain reputation and skill in training, it's a good place to gain a foundation and then go out to other areas or institutions for work. An internship at the Smithsonian will go a long way in securing employment elsewhere. He believes that because of the Smithsonian's size, sometimes really interesting work gets done in smaller museums with a more fixed mission.

Salaries at the Smithsonian

A beginning curator who has almost completed a Ph.D. would earn somewhere in the high-twenties. The next jump would be to the mid-thirties. Staff at the Smithsonian are employees of the federal government and follow the GS scale.

What It's Really Like: Researchers in Living History Museums

Researchers are the backbone behind every living history museum. Without their efforts, the ability to recreate authentic period characters, to accurately restore historic buildings, or to reproduce a facsimile of daily life would be an impossible task.

Carolyn Travers, Director of Research, Plimoth Plantation

"We have four sites at Plimoth Plantation: the 1627 Pilgrim Village; the *Mayflower II*; Hobbamock's Homesite, a Wampanoag Indian dwelling; and the Carriage House Crafts Center. We research anything we need for our program: what is the period attitude toward toads, how a character felt about being her husband's third wife, the correct way to cook a particular dish, or some obscure point of Calvinist theology. The women are more difficult to research than the men because there is less documented information on them. You are forced into recreating a more typical persona than the actual character, sort of a generic portrayal. In general, we research the life and genealogical background and social history for all the characters we portray.

"In our research we use a variety of sources—court records and genealogical research done by professional genealogists such as the General Society of Mayflower Descendants or writers for the *American Genealogist* or other genealogy periodicals.

"We also have researchers in other departments. For example, the authenticity of buildings and structures is done more by our curatorial department."

Carolyn Travers's Background

Carolyn Travers attended Earlham College, a small Quaker school in Richmond, Indiana, where she earned a B.A. in fine arts with a concentration in history. She then went on to Simmons Graduate School of Library and Information Science in Boston and graduated in 1981 with an M.S. in library and information science with a concentration in research methods.

Carolyn Travers grew up in Plymouth and started work at the age of fourteen as a part-time Pilgrim. After she finished her master's degree, she returned to Plimoth Plantation as a researcher.

Qualifications

Carolyn Travers points out that researching is a competitive field and that a higher degree, in history or library science with a research methods concentration, is necessary. A candidate is not expected to have a general body of knowledge about the specific time period, but he or she must have strong research skills, talent, and experience.

Salaries

New graduates might begin with a salary as low as the mid-teens. "You don't do it for the money," Carolyn Travers stresses. "There are a lot of psychological payments. One of the satisfactions is to be able to change someone's mind about the stereotypes surrounding early colonists."

Researchers can find work in a variety of other settings as well: university archaeology and history departments, preservation boards, libraries and archives, government offices, and history museums.

Training Options

How you proceed will depend upon your interests and circumstances. If you are clear from the start what avenue you wish to pursue, you can tailor make a course of study for yourself at the university of your choosing. Courses you'll take or the degree toward which you'll work will depend in part on whether you are a new student or you are already a museum professional making a mid-career change.

Traditionally, new hires to the field of museum work have completed bachelor's and master's degrees in academic disciplines appropriate to the intended career. Curators for art museums have studied art and art history; curators for natural history museums have studied biology, anthropology, archaeology, and so on. And while such a background still serves as the main foundation for successful museum work, for the last thirty years or so more and more people have explored university programs offering practical and theoretical training in the area of museum studies. Courses such as museum management, curatorship, fund-raising, exhibition development, and law and museums offer a more specific approach to the work at hand. This, coupled with a broad background in liberal arts or specialization in an academic discipline, provides museum professionals with a base of knowledge better designed to serve the needs of the museum.

Whatever your course of study, these days most museums require an upper-level degree, either in an academic discipline or in museum studies, museum science, or museology. Also required is an intensive internship or record of long-term volunteer work.

What follows are three possible tracks with which a student can proceed to prepare for a career in museums:

Track 1: *Bachelor's degree* in general museum studies, museology, or museum science. *Master's degree* or *doctorate* in a specific academic discipline. *Internship* arranged through the university or directly with a museum in a particular field.

Track 2: *Bachelor's degree* in liberal arts or a specific academic discipline. *Master's degree* or certificate in museum studies, museology, or museum science. *Internship* arranged through the university or directly with a museum in a particular field.

Track 3: (for the museum professional changing careers or upgrading skills) *Master's degree* or *certificate* in museum studies or *noncredit certificate* in museum studies (short-term course).

The internship is considered the most crucial practical learning experience and is generally a requirement in all programs. The internship can run from ten weeks to a year with varying time commitments per week.

Further Reading

The American Association of Museums (AAM) puts out a publication called the *Guide to Museum Studies & Training in the United States*. It lists more than eighty museum studies programs offering undergraduate or graduate courses or both. Most of these programs came into existence after 1975, and many new programs continue to join the ranks each year.

Some of the undergraduate programs offer only a single overview course supplemented by practica or internships. Many of the graduate programs require the successful completion of six or more courses in addition to the internship.

The guide presents information about a variety of training programs and lists them by state as well as by discipline. Information about pursuing careers in the following areas is also included:

- Archival Management

- Arts Management—Degree Programs

- Arts Management—Nondegree Programs

- Conservation Training—Graduate Programs

- Conservation Training—Nondegree Programs

- Historic Preservation Programs

- Internship or Fellowship Without a Degree

- Internship or Fellowship as Part of a Degree program

- Mid-Career Training Opportunities

- Museum Studies—Bachelor's Degree

- Museum Studies—Certificate

- Museum Studies—Graduate Programs

- Nonprofit Management Programs

- Philanthropy, Volunteerism, and Nonprofit Programs

The Official Museum Directory, put together by the AAM and published by MacMillan Directory Division, is a valuable resource found in the reference section of most libraries. In addition to its pages and pages of history museums, historic houses, buildings, and sites, it lists scores of historical and preservation societies, boards, agencies, councils, commissions, foundations, and research industries. You could decide on a region where you'd like to work, then approach your choices with a phone call, resume and cover letter, or personal visit.

The AAM also puts out a monthly newsletter called *Aviso*. At least half of each issue is devoted to listings for employment opportunities and internships.

In addition to *Guide to Museum Studies & Training in the United States*, the following three reports are put out by the American Association of Museums. They may be ordered by writing:

American Association of Museums
Attn: Bookstore
P.O. Box 40
Washington, DC 20042

1. *Careers in Museums: A Variety of Vocations*. Gives a broad overview of professional career opportunities in museums, suggests educational qualifications and experience for specific positions, and provides information on how to obtain internships. It also lists job placement resources.

2. *Museum Studies Programs: Guide to Evaluation*. Answers questions about the curriculum and quality of museum studies programs that you have already identified.

3. *Museum Studies Programs in the United States: A Resource Guide*. Provides information on training opportunities,

internships and fellowships, mid-career opportunities, and management programs.

Another useful book that you may be able to find at your local public library is *Introduction to Museum Work*, by G. Ellis Burcaw. For museum workers worldwide, it covers collections, interpretation, educational programs, and exhibits.

CHAPTER EIGHT

Botanical Specialists

Botanical gardens and arboreta are parks open to the general public, students, and research scientists. Plants, flowers, trees, and shrubs are collected from all over the world and exhibited in arrangements by family, country of origin, or with regard to aesthetics.

Typical visitors to botanical gardens and arboreta fall into six categories: dedicated professional scientists and horticulturists who utilize the gardens' collections for research purposes or to identify specific plants; professional and amateur gardeners who participate in adult education classes and training programs; horticultural students enrolled in internship programs through their universities; local residents who come to enjoy a peaceful sanctuary; schoolchildren and their teachers; and international travelers and scientists interested in the collections and histories of the gardens.

Botanical gardens and arboreta generally offer public programs such as classes in gardening, question and answer hot lines to help with gardening problems, tours of the grounds, and lectures on the various collections.

Although not all, most botanical gardens and arboreta are involved with ongoing research issues. Curators and other horticulturists go on collection trips to add to the types of plants in their gardens and to study the plant life in other geographic regions.

Living plants are added to the grounds, and pressed and dried plants are stored in herbaria and are shared with researchers all over the world.

Jobs and Salaries Within Botanical Gardens and Arboreta

Within botanical gardens and arboreta are many positions that would be of interest to scholars. Although job titles can vary from institution to institution, some of the common designations follow, along with typical salaries. Keep in mind, though, that the geographic region, the size and budget of the institution, and the experience of the applicant will all determine actual salaries, which could be far greater (or lower) than these averages.

Position	Job Description	Salary
Administration, Facilities, Security		
Director	Provides leadership and is responsible for policy making, funding, planning, organizing, staffing, and directing activities throughout the institution.	$48,000
Assistant Director	Responsible for operations, which may include finance, personnel, and maintenance of facilities, security, and safety.	$40,000
Business Manager	Responsible for accounting, payroll and benefits, purchasing, personnel, and financial record keeping.	$32,190
Store Manager	Manages the institution's gift shop or store.	$22,000
Security Officer	Guards property against theft, illegal entry, fire, and vandalism. Enforces rules and regulations, protects visitors, and may be required to administer first aid.	$20,280

Position	Job Description	Salary

Horticulture, Curation of Collections

Position	Job Description	Salary
Head of Horticulture	Directs the horticultural function of the institution, including the management of staff, programs, activities, and plant collections.	$31,100
Curator/Horticulture	Advises on care of plant collections and acquisitions.	$28,180
Plant Records Keeper	Maintains inventory of plants. Processes acquisitions, accession and deaccession, mapping, relocating, and labeling.	$23,675
Production Supervisor	Supervises the growing of plants in the nursery.	$23,900
Propagator	Propagates plant materials for collections.	$22,775

Grounds Management

Position	Job Description	Salary
Horticulture Supervisor	Supervises garden workers, plans and schedules work assignments, and is responsible for equipment.	$27,000
Foreman	Directs laborer crews in general groundskeeping tasks.	$23,500
Laborer:	Maintains general grounds.	$17,470
Gardener	Responsible for the maintenance of a specialized plant area or collection.	$21,254
Arborist	Responsible for the care of trees, including trimming, transplanting, and removal.	$21,254

Position	Job Description	Salary
Education, Visitor Services		
Head of Education	Responsible for several departments or programs. Supervises several education professionals and/or volunteers.	$29,000
Education Specialist	Responsible for a specific program. Supervises staff related to that program.	$23,650
Visitor Services Manager	Coordinates informational programs and services.	$24,460

What It's Really Like

Rick Darke, Curator of Plants at Longwood Gardens

Longwood Gardens is located in Kennett Square, Pennsylvania, a suburb of Philadelphia. Curator of plants, Rick Darke, explains its function:

"We're not really a botanic garden; we're a display garden, a pleasure garden. We have quite a few plants that could be called collections, but they exist for the sake of the landscape texture. That's how we differ from a traditional botanical garden. We have a lot more emphasis on the art of the landscape, the pleasure derived by people being in that landscape, than we have people coming to study these plants as objects.

"A botanical garden is usually a garden whose primary emphasis is collecting plants, keeping data on them for the purpose of display and study.

"Pierre Dupont, the founder of Longwood Gardens, was interested in creating a mood and a sense of place that would allow people to interact within a garden setting. Even though he had a lot of unusual and great specimens, his main emphasis was on the art of horticulture and the setting he was creating. At a botanical garden they worry secondly how well the spaces work for art or entertainment.

"We do have a research division at Longwood within our horticultural division, but our research is not at the micro level. In other words, we're not doing research on projects useful only in laboratory settings or that would not have much practical applicability. What we're trying to do is bring science to bear on display horticulture. We do have true Ph.D. scientists in our division, but they're here to use their knowledge of science to help us be efficient, imaginative, and responsible to the environment in our fabricating of plant displays.

"It's a historic garden in some sense. There was an arboretum here started by a Quaker family who got the land from a grant from William Penn, whom Pennsylvania is named for. They planted trees in the 1780s that are still existing today, and it was that core arboretum that was the compelling factor in Pierre Dupont's decision to buy the property. The trees were due to be logged, and Dupont bought the land to save them. He fell in love with the place and over the years developed Longwood Gardens around it.

"Pierre Dupont was an engineer who had a love of water in the garden, so he built fountain gardens that were inspired by his visits to Europe. These are major attractions. We also have a theater garden with live performances. The curtain is a curtain of water jets.

"There's also a topiary garden of abstract shapes and lots of wonderful old trees, grand vistas, and monumental architecture at the conservatories, with bronze windows and mica-shaded lamps inside.

"We intend it to be gorgeous, and I think we succeed. We wow people in a very classy way."

Rick Darke's Duties as Curator of Plants

Longwood Gardens has a little over a thousand acres, about one-fourth of which are accessible to the public. Of these, about eighty acres are actually display gardens.

Rick Darke has been at Longwood Gardens for close to eighteen years. He talks about his job: "I'm a plantsman for Longwood, someone who is knowledgeable about the diversity of plants that exists in the world, because we grow plants from the world over. First and foremost, if there is any one thing that has to get done here, it's keeping everything at Longwood identified and labeled, and that's the most important thing. I organize and oversee the identification, mapping, and labeling that is done by the curatorial assistants I supervise.

"I also have a very steady role in making recommendations and working in team settings to make and refine and restore the gardens at Longwood. To that end, I participate regularly on landscape and advisory committees. My role is to suggest plants we could use in place of what we're using now, or sometimes it overlaps into related areas. I'm often making comments on architectural details or labeling and other interpretive details.

"I also get to travel a lot looking for new plants for Longwood. I've traveled to Australia, New Zealand, Japan, South Africa, Brazil, England, Germany. I bring back beautiful plants from all kinds of climates. We have four acres under glass here so we can grow things that are hardy, and we can also create specialized environments that provide the essentials of the environments the plants are from.

"I do quite a bit of teaching; it's a considerable part of the job. We have a lot of different student programs here and I regularly teach a botany course for our PG (Professional Gardener) students and other classes for our graduate student program. I teach courses for our continuing education program, which includes evening lectures and field trips. I lead tours to native areas and other gardens.

"I also write. I contribute to our in-house publication, which is essentially a record of the employees and happenings around the garden, and I also write magazine articles on what Longwood is doing. For example, when I went to Brazil I worked with a landscape architect there and brought him back to Longwood. He made a garden for us, and I wrote an article on that. I worked with our photographer to get that published. It's a celebration of the gardens at Longwood."

Rick is a member of the Garden Writers Association of America and is the author of *For Your Garden: Ornamental Grasses* (Little, Brown).

The eclectic mix of his job and the interaction he gets to have with students is what Rick likes most about his work. "We usually have an intern in our office, and I'm constantly teaching people as they move through the organization. Over the years, you can imagine the wonderful network you make of friends and professional colleagues around the country and the world.

"In my job, I get to do something that's fun. It's not just going to work at eight and ending at five. It's much more than that. It really is something that teaches you. I have become in these past eighteen years someone who loves his garden at home. I'm out there digging and planting and designing, and it's gotten to the point that features of the garden are publishable, and it provides a source of photography. All of that has become a wonderful enrichment that comes from my job. Because it's so close to what I would do if I just had the time to play, it blurs the line between vocation and avocation."

Do You Have What It Takes?

Rick Darke suggests that the following skills, in addition to a love of plants, are necessary for success in his profession: "You need good writing skills and verbal communication. I could not do what I do, and I would not have had the opportunities, if I hadn't worked on being able to articulate my notions."

Rick Darke's Background

Rick has a bachelor's degree in plant sciences from the University of Delaware. "I took a circuitous route. I spent seven years as an undergraduate and went through art and anthropology on the way to plant science. Longwood was my first job. I started as an intern there, then moved into an assistant taxonomist position. I did go back and take some graduate courses in plant systematics and taxonomy. However, instead of going back and completing a graduate degree, it worked to my advantage to stay here. I ended up taking over a Ph.D. position in taxonomy that was rewritten as a curator of plants. The man I was working for was due to retire in two years, and it was a question of would I learn more by staying on the job and developing the skills I'd need to take over, or would I learn more by getting into a graduate program. My choice to stay worked out."

Anne Brennan, Student Intern

Anne Brennan graduated from Penn State with a B.S. in horticulture and worked at Longwood Gardens doing a postgraduate internship in the education division. It was a ten-month paid internship that provided a monthly stipend of $800 and free housing. It also gave Anne a chance to experience different career options to help her decide what she would like to do.

"I started out thinking about horticultural production, growing the plants, as a possible career, whether in a greenhouse or nursery, but then I realized that there are so many more options out there. Here at Longwood Gardens I see new possibilities every day.

"When I was in school, I wasn't even aware that botanical gardens existed. Public gardens were not emphasized at my university. But they're very big, especially in the United States. There are botanical gardens everywhere, and they all have horticulturists. They all have education people, publicists, and all different sorts of positions that are filled with people with horticultural backgrounds.

"I think I didn't know about it mainly because people teaching in universities have, of course, gone to graduate school and done research, and that's what they see as horticulture, the academic and research end of things or the production end of things. That's what direction a lot of them were pushed in, without even realizing it. My advisor kept mentioning grad school, but I was never very excited about it; I didn't see how it would fit in for me. Now that I'm out of school and interacting with people who didn't all follow that path, I see other options.

"My job here is unique because I work in the student programs office, which is the office that coordinates the internship program, as well as a two-year program called the professional gardener training program, and also an international student internship program with five students. So, I'm an intern coordinating other interns.

"It's very interesting. I'm working on a lot of different projects, a lot of day-to-day answering questions from people who are interested in the program. They call or write letters requesting information, and I answer their requests.

"I'm also working on rewriting the promotional material on the three internship programs, and I organize the orientation program for the new interns. I arrange for different people to speak to the students, I give them a tour of the grounds, and I organize field trips to other botanical gardens.

"My job involves a lot of communication skills. There are forty students altogether in all different areas of the gardens. We have meetings twice a month, and I write a long newsletter-type memo each week that includes things they need to know, such as upcoming field trips.

"I like getting to meet all the new people who come in—I'm the first person they see when they arrive.

"I think I'm learning a lot of management skills, too. I have to run meetings; being in charge is not always comfortable for me, but I'm getting used to it.

"I'm not exactly sure what I want to do when my internship is over. I am interested in garden writing. I've had a little experience working for a horticultural trade magazine, and I did enjoy that. I don't know much about layout or publishing, but I'm eager to learn.

"And I really enjoy what I'm doing here working in the education program of a public garden. That's also something I'd like to pursue as a full-time career.

"It would be nice to be able to land in a job as soon as I leave here, but it probably won't happen that way. The job I'm doing now is strictly an intern position, so unless something else opens up, I'll have to move on."

The Arnold Arboretum

The Arnold Arboretum is located in Jamaica Plain, Massachusetts, a section of Boston, and is affiliated with Harvard University. Its mission is the biology, cultivation, and conservation of temperate woody plants. Within that mission fall the goals of continuing research, education, and community outreach work.

The Arnold Arboretum was the brainchild of Harvard botanist Asa Gray. With a bequeath from James Arnold of New Bedford and help from the will's trustees, Gray was able to realize his dream.

The Arnold Arboretum started with 123 species of neglected woody plants in 1874 and has since grown to 265 beautifully maintained acres, with approximately 15,000 plants in its living collection.

Chris Strand, Outreach Horticulturist

Chris Strand is an outreach horticulturist at the Arnold Arboretum. He earned his bachelor's degree in biology from the University of Colorado, Boulder, in 1989, focusing on taxonomy, the study of the different species and how they are classified.

After he graduated, he won a fellowship sponsored by Longwood Gardens and earned his master's degree in public horticulture at the University of Delaware in Newark. He worked for one year at Callaway Gardens near Atlanta, Georgia, then started with the Arnold Arboretum in 1993.

"I'm in charge of visitor services, and under that I have a wide range of duties. I develop and manage the exhibits that go in our exhibit hall. That's where all the information is disseminated to visitors. It's small—the real exhibit is the 265 acres of grounds that make up the arboretum—but in the exhibit hall we have an information desk and photographs and a bookstore with books on woody plants for sale.

"I have to make sure there are volunteers stationed in the exhibit hall to answer visitors' questions, and I train the volunteers so they know how to answer the questions.

"I make sure the bookstore buyer has everything she needs; I make sure there are maps of the grounds available so that people can navigate around the landscape. I put together lists of what's in flower and post upcoming events.

"On a typical day, I make sure the exhibit hall is in shape, and then I work on any number of projects. Right now I'm involved with putting together a map of the great trees of the arboretum. We have about fifteen thousand, and I choose a few that people would be interested in seeing and put them in a brochure. I also coordinate the volunteers, and I have a couple of high school students who are helping with the project.

"On any given day, I also teach classes; I'm an instructor in the adult education program. I cover woody plant identification and I teach a six-week course on the highlights of the arboretum. My students are interested in continuing education; they are retired people, volunteers wanting to learn more about the plants, or rangers from the National Park Service.

"We have a cooperative arrangement with the National Park Service. Interpretative rangers used to be stationed here to conduct tours on the historical design of the landscape. Now, we're teaching them how to do historical landscape restoration and maintenance. We deal mostly with woody plants and how to replace one as it grows older, maintaining the spirit of the landscape.

"I'm also working on ground signage. Right now there's nothing on the grounds to direct people except for two 'You Are Here' maps. It's been an ongoing project. We have a consultant I work with on that.

"I also answer requests for information on the arboretum and request for publications. I have volunteers who run a plant answer line once a week, so I supply them with all the books they need. They answer probably forty questions a day during the spring.

"But, best of all, I get to spend a lot of time out in the collections. My boss has made it clear that I'm supposed to be very familiar with everything, so I spend a lot of time going outside looking at plants, photographing them, learning about them. We have more than eleven thousand different specimens on the grounds, and the best part is that I always have the opportunity to learn more about them.

"The worst part is dealing with some difficult people. We are a public park, and we don't charge admission. Some people disregard the rules. For example, they bring their dogs in and don't clean up after them or keep them leashed. We had a family of goslings, but there's only one left now because the retrievers fetch them.

"There have been people who have vandalized the property or who have clipped all the peonies to sell on the street corner. The Boston park rangers patrol the grounds, but they can't be everywhere at once."

Climbing the Career Ladder in Public Horticulture

Graduate programs in public horticulture are directed toward people who are interested in working in education or administration. Chris Strand tells us his future career plans:

"I think I'll continue to work in some sort of public program. Eventually I'd like to be in charge of a public program at an arboretum or botanic garden, moving up the ladder on the same track I'm on now.

"But I hope I'll always be able to have contact with the plants because that's the best part of the job. The more administrative your position, the less contact you have."

Susan Kelley, Curatorial Associate

Susan Kelley is a curatorial associate for the living collections at Arnold Arboretum. Her job involves mapping the living specimens on the grounds and labeling each plant.

"We're more than a horticultural garden," she explains. "Our collections are used scientifically. We have a lot of visitors from all over the world who use our collections for study. Maps showing where each individual plant is on the grounds have been kept since the 1930s.

"Right now we're in the process of switching from a series of about a hundred hand-drawn maps to a computerized mapping system using computer-aided design. We're honing down to about sixty-five maps plus insets. My job is not only to transcribe the hand-drawn maps to the computerized but also to maintain current hand-drawn maps in the interim. We have two major plantings a year, in the spring and in the fall, and probably a thousand new plants go out every year onto the grounds. My job is to put the new plantings on the maps.

"I also field check each individual specimen for condition. If it's damaged, I let the propagator know it might need to be re-propagated. I recommend to the horticultural taxonomist or the superintendent of the grounds if something needs to be removed. The plant could be dying, diseased, or suffering damage from the weather or vandalism.

"I'm also responsible for making sure that every plant is labeled. The labels are hung directly on the plant. Each plant is supposed to have two records labels that give an accession number, the name of the plant, the family, where it came from, and the map location.

"When a plant goes from the nursery to the grounds, I take over and maintain the records on each plant. We have about fifteen thousand on the grounds now. My boss is the horticultural taxonomist, and we work very closely together. He decides what goes out on the grounds every spring and fall, assessing what's in the nursery and what will be planted. He puts together the planting bulletins, which are then handed to me. I use those to map the new plantings.

"And I'm supposed to be able to identify everything. Labels do get lost sometimes or switched by the public. If there are any problems and I can't figure out what a plant is, for example, I ask him. There are specific plant families he's interested in, and people from all over the world send him things to identify.

"The labels I'm responsible for are the size of a credit card and are made out of anodized aluminum. We gather the information on the plant from our computer's database and lay it out with the correct number of lines and spaces. We have an embossing machine that actually prints out the label.

"Seventy percent of my time is spent outdoors, even in the winter. I have a lot of mapping and record keeping to do then. It's a great time to field check the conifer collection, the pines, the firs, the spruce, and so on. You can also find labels more easily when there aren't any leaves on the trees, because they're hung above the ground level. With shrubs, though, it's a disaster to find the labels when there's snow on the ground."

Susan Kelley's Background

Susan started out as a violinist and earned both bachelor's and master's degrees in music before she decided to switch careers.

"I was freelancing in New York, and it was a difficult life. I had plenty of work, but everyone was so unhappy living there. Plants had always been an interest of mine growing up in Tennessee, and I loved gardening.

"I went back to school at City University of New York and got my master's in plant population ecology.

"I worked at the Harvard University Herbaria in Cambridge for a while as a partial employee of Arnold Arboretum. So, naturally I met people from the Arnold Arboretum; they would come to Cambridge, I would go to Jamaica Plain. When my current position became available, I applied. I prefer being outdoors as opposed to working indoors all day.

"Because of the relationship of Harvard and the arboretum, we are all technically employees of Harvard—and we get all the benefits of a Harvard employee. We can take courses for $40, for example, and there are excellent health benefits, life insurance, and a free pass to all the museums in Boston and the surrounding area."

The Pluses and Minuses of Susan's Job

"What I love most is being outdoors in this great collection of plants. It's one of the best collections in the world. There are very old specimens, and then we have all these new plants coming in. I also like that I have some indoor work. The computer work I do is challenging mentally. The mix is ideal.

"The only stress I have is that we're understaffed, and my job is extensive enough that three people should really be doing it. I do have volunteers I coordinate, and I have two interns in the summertime who help. But managing people can also add to the stress. You have to take the time to train them, and it's extra work. We get applicants from all over the world for the internship program here, and we don't interview in person. It's always tricky to interview someone over the phone and try to get an idea how they would work out. But whenever I need to regroup I can just go outside. I have a beautiful place in which to do it."

The Career Ladder for Mappers and Labelers

"This is a great job; I could feasibly stay here for a long time. There's so much more to learn. For example, there's another mapping system I'm interested in—GIS, Geographic Information System.

"With more experience, more study and research and publications, one could move up into a curatorial position. I'd want to become more proficient with taxonomic work and go on collecting trips. We have a research program in Indonesia, and I'd love to go there one day and do mapping at the botanical gardens."

Internships at Botanical Gardens and Arboreta

"Horticulture is an occupation you can't learn by just being in the classroom," says Dave Foresman, student programs coordinator at Longwood Gardens. "You have to have work experience and on-the-job training. We would not hire anybody without work experience, whether it's summer work or a bona fide internship program. This is very important."

Most public gardens offer some sort of student internship program, though the programs might differ in the degrees of responsibility the interns have and the departments in which they could be placed.

"Longwood's internships differ quite a bit from those with other botanical gardens," Dave explains. "We're providing gardening experience. We have people in other divisions, but most of our interns are working either outside in the gardens or in the conservatories doing the same kind of work our gardeners are doing each day. They're learning those skills, the equipment, methods, and procedures used in public display facilities.

"In other gardens, internships might provide more responsibility. A student could be rotated throughout various work areas. Our interns apply and are chosen for a specific location. For example, if they elect a flower garden internship, they will stay in that division throughout the internship. There might be eight to ten stations you might work at in the flower garden, but you wouldn't normally come in and work in the greenhouse or in research.

"You can't become a botanist or curator without becoming a gardener first. You have to know the basic techniques."

Internships can run from three months to a year. Usually interns are juniors or seniors in college or are recent graduates. Interns work from thirty-five to forty hours per week and can be placed in any department within the botanical garden or arboretum.

Some gardens offer professional gardener programs. Longwood's program is a two-year stint combining academics and hands-on training.

"Students in this program move around to different departments on a scheduled rotation," Dave Foresman explains. "These are paid positions with housing. Students spent ten hours a week in the classroom for a two-year period and twenty-five hours a week receiving hands-on training.

"Graduates from our professional gardener program are very much sought after. The program is twenty-four years old, and we've had only 137 graduates in that time. Just this morning we had two job offerings that came in by phone. We post fifty to seventy-five jobs a year, and we graduate only about fourteen students every other year."

Internships at some gardens are very competitive. Longwood has only forty slots for the student internship program but receives more than a hundred applications a year.

To find the internship or professional gardener program that's right for you, you can contact the garden of your choice directly or go through your university department's internship office.

There is also a directory of more than five hundred internships and summer programs published by the American Association of Botanical Gardens and Arboreta (AABGA).

Further Reading

The following resources are publications of the American Association of Botanical Gardens and Arboreta (AABGA) and can be ordered directly from the association at:

American Association of Botanical Gardens and
    Arboreta (AABGA)
786 Church Road
Wayne, PA 19087

Salary Survey contains the latest salary and benefit information for twenty-two positions in administration, horticulture, and education at U.S. and Canadian botanical gardens.

Internship Directory lists more than five hundred summer jobs and internships at 125 botanical gardens, arboreta, and other horticultural institutions. Includes positions in grounds management, education, collections, curation, and more.

A *Directory of Volunteer Programs at Public Gardens* profiles 121 volunteer programs at public gardens, listing volunteer services, special events, and the addresses and telephone numbers for volunteer coordinators.

CHAPTER NINE

Animal Behaviorists

Just as scholars satisfy their curiosity and find fulfilling careers studying humans, plants, and information in general, there is a whole realm of professionals who study animal behavior as well. The ideal animal behaviorist is someone who has experience handling animals and who is professionally trained in the areas of the scientific analysis of behavior, as well as being trained to counsel people about animals.

Becoming an Animal Behaviorist

The ability to think critically is probably one of the most valuable assets an animal behaviorist should have. That also includes the ability to evaluate—to be able to tell what the results you see mean and to evaluate them without reference to your personal prejudices.

Most animal behaviorists earn a doctorate degree in animal behavior programs in university psychology or zoology departments. They also must combine hands-on experience with their research interests.

What It's Really Like

Mary Lee Nitschke, Animal Behaviorist

Mary Lee Nitschke has a Ph.D. in comparative developmental psychobiology from Michigan State University and more than thirty years experience in this exciting field. "For someone who wants to become an animal behaviorist, first of all, you have to have hands-on experience," she explains, "and the more time you spend observing animals and learning how to interact with them, the better off you're going to be. The second thing is that you have to get educated to learn to understand, evaluate, and think like a scientist.

"Hands-on experience is very important. I don't think this is a profession that can be done totally by theory. On the other hand, the hands-on experience can't come totally from trial and error methods.

"I think the best approach is to take a lot of experimental courses—psychology or in other fields. Some anthropology courses do a good job of preparing people. There are disciplines of animal behavior both within psychology and zoology. I think that a good psychology background is important, not just for experimental psych, but if you take a major in psychology in almost any school in the country, you will have to take experimental psychology and statistics. Applied statistics is something I use on a daily basis. I'll give you an example. Every time a client comes in to me and says 'this is happening.' In my mind I run that through a statistical analysis, and I say, given that situation, what is the probability this is happening for these reasons. That's where my training and my knowledge of animal behavior allows me to put that in a framework instantly."

Dr. Nitschke wears many hats. She is a full-time, tenured professor in the psychology department at Linfield College in Portland, Oregon. There she teaches a variety of courses, from Applied Animal Behavior and Human Animal Relationships to People Pet Partnerships in Health Care.

She is owner of Animal School Incorporated (in Beaverton, Oregon) and, through private consultations and classes, provides clients with help in solving pet behavior problems.

Here is an example of the kinds of problems she sees. "Recently, a fellow came in with a six-year-old bulldog mix. It looked an awful lot like a pit bull. Big dog, ninety pounds, and he has bitten about seven people. I went through each bite. Some of these bites are almost to be expected because they resulted from inappropriate behavior on the part of the owner. In one instance, the owner sent a plumber carrying a pipe into the dog's territory without announcing him. Well, he already knew the dog was territorial and didn't usually admit strangers. I don't count that bite. That was to be expected. In another instance, a teenage boy had been playing with the dog, then turned very abruptly and jumped on his bike, and the dog went for him. Given this particular dog, the probability of that happening is pretty high, and, when you add all those bites up, the probability that the dog is going to bite again is also very high. Putting the dog to sleep is one of the major options I counseled him about, but you can't make that decision for the client. My job in that situation is to say, here are the likely scenarios—what will happen if you do nothing or if you do this, that, or the other.

"What he wanted from me was to give him a training program that would guarantee that the dog wouldn't bite anyone again. But there is no such program. Most of the time you're working with the person, not the animal, and that's why you must have some grounding in counseling to do this work."

Dr. Nitschke is also a consultant to the Oregon Zoo in Portland. "The Oregon Zoo employs a full-time animal behaviorist. I work on a consulting basis with her, doing training seminars for zookeepers on how to interact with and handle animals.

"I also give talks on wolf-dog crosses because the zoo gets questions about them all the time. The zoo has wolves, so people come to them with their concerns about their own pets, and they want to know how to answer the questions. The Northwest is a hotbed for people owning wolves as pets. It's pretty hard on everyone, though it doesn't keep people from doing it. From a wolf-dog cross, the biggest problem I see professionally is the quality of life for that animal. If it's high percentage wolf, it's likely to be terrified of people. The second problem is its unpredictability. We have no way of knowing when the wolf part is going to be operative and when the dog part is. These wolf-dog crosses have a rap very similar to pit bulls and rottweilers. It's not the same problem at all, but it looks like the same problem because they maul children frequently.

"I also do training with the zookeepers, teaching them how to manage animals in the zoo environment and how to understand and use operant behavior and clicker training. The animal is trained to click a bar that will deliver food to it as a reward. One of my colleagues was working with an ape that was diabetic and needed to have a blood sample drawn every day. Through clicker training, she taught the chimp to put its arm in a sleeve outside the cage and grasp a bar so that the blood sample could be taken quickly and efficiently without anybody being endangered. The reward was food, and the animal was fine about it.

"Another one she did was to teach an elephant to present its feet for cleaning through the fence. This was an aggressive male elephant, and nobody could go in and do this. Through operant conditioning, it was taught to hold its feet up to a little panel, and then they could be cleaned that way.

"I also worked with one of the birds of prey that wouldn't allow keepers in, so we did some work with that. Basically, when they have a problem they call me."

In addition, Dr. Nitschke does a lot of public speaking and is also a consultant for the invisible fencing industry. "Those are the major things," Dr. Nitschke explains, "but other things come up. I do training for the animal-control people sometimes. I train them on how to handle animals, how to approach an animal when they have to go onto a property—because that's one of the most dangerous jobs in the world, going onto an animal's property and trying to pick it up."

Mary Lee Nitschke's Background

"I grew up on the range in Texas, and my major entertainment and stimulation came from observing animals. One of my earliest memories is lying in the grass watching bobwhite quail coming to drink water in the summer. My young life was devoted to animals.

"I had spent a lot time with animals, horses especially, both showing them and training them, and when I got to college I was attracted to both engineering psychology—because I was in love with machines—and animal behavior.

"What I thought was so interesting, and what has fueled me throughout life in some ways, was that the theoretical stuff I was learning in college, theories of psychology and learning theory, seemed to me to be wasted if it wasn't applied. Yet my professors knew nothing about training, and here we were discussing learning theory. And, by the same token, trainers knew nothing about learning theory. I couldn't imagine that both of these areas couldn't be enriched by the other, so I kept bouncing back and forth between what was going on in the training world and what was going on in learning theory in the academic world. And then when I got to grad school and discovered I could actually study this as an academic subject, too, I was just fascinated with putting that together.

"Most of my research in graduate school was aimed at the 'interspecific communication of distress.' In my dissertation, I did research with bobwhite quail, jackrabbits, coyotes, blue jays, and human babies. What I was looking for was whether there was some universality of understanding of the distress call between species.

"After I graduated, I taught at Michigan State University. I taught operant behavior, among other things, then I taught pet communication patterns in the veterinary school there. I also taught developmental psychobiology with a specialization in toxicology—again looking across species—what are the common elements in how toxins affect behavior in various species.

"Before I even went to college, I trained horses. What I later realized is that I trained every animal I came into contact with—I just didn't realize that's what it was called.

"While I was an undergraduate, one of the things that fueled my interest in applied psychology was that I started out working in a kennel that bred and trained collies. It was really one of the golden fortunes of my life that the couple I worked for had incredible integrity and ethics about breeding. They bred for the love of the dog and could not be bought by local fashions and current fads. They knew exactly what they were breeding for—solid temperaments. I learned an incredible amount from them. I started there just cleaning dog runs, and by the time I left I was handling the line of collies professionally."

Career Options

Independent Trainers

Just as Dr. Nitschke does, many animal behaviorists work independently and offer training programs to pet owners. Dr. Nitschke admits that getting started can be difficult. "Your best referral sources are veterinarians. People in the United States think that veterinarians are the pet gods, and so they ask them everything. If you don't have the support of the veterinarians in your local community, you're going to have a rough go of it. You have to advertise and market yourself."

Teaching

Many animal behaviorists stay in the academic world, where they pass on their experience and research to university-level students. Just as with any professorial post, you would need to have your doctorate and to meet the specific requirements of the hiring department.

Animal-Assisted Therapy

Another arena in which people work is animal-assisted therapy. Dr. Nitschke explains: "Animal-assisted therapy is where the animals become part of the therapeutic process. They can be used with people with a wide range of problems, anything from a social dog for a child who maybe has emotional or social problems up through people who need the dog as a prosthesis, such as Seeing Eye, hearing ear, or seizure alert dogs, for example. Animal behaviorists train animals for these roles."

Dr. Nitschke teaches others about hippotherapy and how to work with horses to help humans with neuromuscular difficulties. "I hope I'm carving out a path that will become more common as the years go by—teaching people to use animals therapeutically. One of these programs is called People Pet Partnerships in Health Care.

"Hippotherapy is horseback riding directed by a physical therapist or a kinesiologist. The movement of the horse is used as a way of stimulating neuromuscular interaction patterns with the person. My mission with this course is to teach people in the medical field some of the wonderful possibilities that are available therapeutically with animals.

"Another application is showcased by the work of Dr. Mary Birch. She works with crack babies who have no inhibitory control and scream most of the time. Those babies are very hard for the nurses to take care of. It is also very hard to have an impact on them in any way.

"What Dr. Birch did was use a concept called entrainment. You take the rhythm that's occurring in the patient, and you match something to it that will correspond to that rhythm, and then you start bringing it down. She started with little, active, very flighty finches in a cage right next to the baby. The baby is eventually entrained on those finches. Then, what she did was substitute the finches with birds that moved more slowly, to the point where she could finally put a chinchilla in with that baby and it would soothe the baby. It's a combination of biofeedback and animal behavior stuff and circadian rhythm stuff. There are all sorts of ways that, if you understand what is happening with the animal and its behavior, you can use it therapeutically."

Medical Research

As any animal lover knows, research using animals is a controversial subject, to say the least. However, as Dr. Nitschke points out, "anyone developing medications or procedures for animals is going to need the services of someone trained in evaluating behavior at some point—and should. Too often they haven't. What they've typically done is gone to veterinarians who may not have had any training in animal behavior and most often don't." An animal behaviorist working with scientists for the betterment of animals can ensure that humane practices are followed.

Training Trainers

Teaching other people how to train animals is a viable career path for animal behaviorists. Although the notion of training animals for circuses or television or film work might be abhorrent to some (there are many who believe that animals should be left in the wild and not used for any purposes related to people's needs), as mentioned earlier, animals can humanely be trained to interact with humans in a therapeutic setting.

"There are a lot of folks out there who still believe that punishment is the most effective and most efficient way to train," says Dr. Nitschke. "If you get a trainer who believes that and also does not have good anger management, then the potential for abuse arises very quickly. I spend a lot of time trying to educate people about what it means to be a humane trainer. What we teach is essentially the same thing that is taught in positive parenting classes. Rewarding good behavior, ignoring the bad. That's traditional behavior modification."

In Zoos

As mentioned earlier, many zoos either hire animal behaviorists or work with consultants to train zookeepers how to handle and interact well with the animals.

More and more zoos operate open park facilities as opposed to keeping animals in cement-floored cages. Animal behaviorists teach zoo owners about the needs of the different animals—for example, which animals can be kept in the same park spaces together and which must be kept separated.

Income for Animal Behaviorists

Salaries would vary widely depending upon the specific work you do and the area in the country in which you live. Those working for a university would expect to be on the same pay scale as any other faculty member of the same rank and experience.

As a consultant and trainer, Mary Lee Nitschke says, "I charge everyone $90 an hour, no matter what I'm doing for them. All my consulting is $90 an hour. I set that fee based on the average fee that psychologists charge in my area. And it's about to go up. I'll probably go up to $100 or a little more than that. Right now, we have about twenty different classes, and the cost is about $85 to $90 for a set of six classes per student."

For more information about animal behavior, see the resources listed in the Appendix.

Professional Associations

F or more information on the career options covered in this book, contact the appropriate professional associations listed below.

College and University Teachers

Professional societies generally provide information on academic and nonacademic employment opportunities in their fields. You can find addresses for professional associations for many academic disciplines in the *Occupational Outlook Handbook*. Another resource is the *Encyclopedia of Associations*, available at your library.

For information about faculty union activities on two- and four-year college campuses, contact:

American Federation of Teachers
555 New Jersey Avenue NW
Washington, DC 20001

For information on college teaching careers, contact:

American Association of University Professors
1012 Fourteenth Street NW
Washington, DC 20005

Special publications on higher education, available in libraries, list specific employment opportunities for faculty. The major periodical is the *Chronicle of Higher Education*.

Librarians and Archivists

Information on librarianship, including a listing of accredited education programs and information on scholarships or loans, is available from:

American Library Association (ALA)
Office for Library Personnel Resources
50 East Huron Street
Chicago, IL 60611

For information on a career as a special librarian, write to:

Special Libraries Association
1700 Eighteenth Street NW
Washington, DC 20009

Material on careers in information science is available from:

American Society for Information Science
8720 Georgia Avenue, Suite 501
Silver Spring, MD 20910

Information on graduate schools of library and information science can be obtained from:

Association for Library and Information Science Education
4101 Lake Boone Trail, Suite 201
Raleigh, NC 27607

Those interested in a position as a librarian in the federal service should write to:

Office of Personnel Management
1900 E Street NW
Washington, DC 20415

Information on schools receiving federal financial assistance for library training is available from:

Office of Educational Research and Improvement
Library Programs
Library Development Staff
U.S. Department of Education
555 New Jersey Avenue NW, Room 402
Washington, DC 20208

For information on a career as a law librarian, as well as a list of ALA accredited library schools offering programs in law librarianship and scholarship information, contact:

American Association of Law Libraries
53 West Jackson Boulevard, Suite 940
Chicago, IL 60604

For information on employment opportunities as a health science librarian, contact:

Medical Library Association
6 North Michigan Avenue, Suite 300
Chicago, IL 60602

Information concerning requirements and application procedures for positions in the Library of Congress may be obtained directly from:

Personnel Office
Library of Congress
101 Independence Avenue SE
Washington, DC 20540

State library agencies can furnish information on scholarships available through their offices, requirements for certification, and general information about career prospects in the state. Several of these agencies maintain job hot lines that report openings for librarians. State departments of education can furnish information on certification requirements and job opportunities for school librarians.

For information on archivists and schools offering courses in archival science, contact:

Society of American Archivists
600 South Federal Street, Suite 504
Chicago, IL 60605

For information about certification for archivists, contact:

Academy of Certified Archivists
600 South Federal Street, Suite 504
Chicago, IL 60605

Genealogists

Board for Certification of Genealogists
P.O. Box 5816
Falmouth, VA 22403

Family History Library
Church of Jesus Christ of Latter-Day Saints
35 Northwest Temple
Salt Lake City, UT 84150

Genealogical Library
Church of Jesus Christ of Latter-Day Saints
35 Northwest Temple
Salt Lake City, UT 84150

National Genealogical Society
4527 Seventeenth Street North
Arlington, VA 22207

Anthropologists

For information about careers, job openings, grants and fellow-ships, and schools that offer training in anthropology, and for a copy of *Getting a Job Outside the Academy* (special publication no. 14), contact:

The American Anthropological Association
4350 North Fairfax Drive, Suite 640
Arlington, VA 22203

Archaeologists

Archaeological Conservancy
415 Orchard Drive
Santa Fe, NM 87501

Archaeological Institute of America
675 Commonwealth Avenue
Boston, MA 02215

Society for American Archaeology
900 Second Street NE, #12
Washington, DC 20002

Geographers

Two publications provide information on careers and job openings for geographers: *Geography Today's Career for Tomorrow*, available free of charge; and *Careers in Geography*, available for a small fee. An annual publication lists schools offering various programs in geography: *A Guide to Programs of Geography in the U.S. and Canada*. These publications may be obtained from:

Association of American Geographers
1710 Sixteenth Street NW
Washington, DC 20009

Historians

Information on careers for students of history is available from:

American Historical Association
400 A Street SE
Washington, DC 20003

General information on careers for historians is available from:

Organization of American Historians
112 North Bryan Street
Bloomington, IN 47408

For additional information on careers for historians, send a self-addressed, stamped envelope to:

American Association for State and Local History
530 Church Street, Sixth Floor
Nashville, TN 37219

Political Scientists

Information on careers and job openings, including *Careers and the Study of Political Science: A Guide for Undergraduates*, available for a small fee, with bulk rates for multiple copies, may be purchased from:

American Political Science Association
1527 New Hampshire Avenue NW
Washington, DC 20036

Programs in Public Affairs and Administration, a biennial directory that contains data on the academic content of programs, the student body, the format of instruction, and other information, may be purchased from:

National Association of Schools of Public Affairs and
   Administration
1120 G Street NW, Suite 730
Washington, DC 20005

Psychologists

For information on careers, educational requirements, financial assistance, and licensing in all fields of psychology, contact:

American Psychological Association
Education in Psychology and Accreditation Offices
Education Directorate
750 First Street NE
Washington, DC 20002

For information on careers, educational requirements, and licensing of school psychologists, contact:

National Association of School Psychologists
8455 Colesville Road, Suite 1000
Silver Spring, MD 20910

Information about state licensing requirements is available from:

Association of State and Provincial Psychology Boards
P.O. Box 4389
Montgomery, AL 36103

Information on traineeships and fellowships also is available from colleges and universities that have graduate departments of psychology.

Curators

The following list of associations can be used as a valuable resource guide in locating additional information about specific careers. Many of the organizations publish newsletters listing job and internship opportunities, and still others offer an employment service to members. A quick look at the organizations' names will give you an idea of how large the scope is that museums cover.

Advisory Council on Historic Preservation
1100 Pennsylvania Avenue NW
Washington, DC 20004

African-American Museum Association
P.O. Box 548
Wilberforce, OH 45384

American Architectural Preservation Group, Inc.
631 Cross Avenue
Los Angeles, CA 90065

American Arts Alliance
1319 F Street NW, Suite 500
Washington, DC 20004

American Association for the Advancement of Science
1333 H Street NW
Washington, DC 20005

American Association for Museum Volunteers
6307 Hardy Drive
McLean, VA 22101

American Association of Museums
P.O. Box 40
Washington, DC 20042

American Institute for Conservation of Historic
   and Artistic Works
1717 K Street NW, Suite 301
Washington, DC 20006

Association for Living Historical Farms
   and Agricultural Museums
National Museum of American History
Smithsonian Institution, Room 5035
Washington, DC 20560

Association of Art Museum Directors
41 East Sixty-fifth Street
New York, NY 10021

Association of College and University Museums and Galleries
c/o University Museum
Southern Illinois University at Edwardsville
Edwardsville, IL 62026

Association of Railway Museums
4131 Franklin Street, Suite 11
San Francisco, CA 94123

Association of Science Museum Directors
c/o National Museum of Natural History
Smithsonian Institution
Washington, DC 20560

Association of Science Technology Centers
1025 Vermont Avenue NW, Suite 500
Washington, DC 20005

Association of Systematics Collections
(Natural History Museums)
730 Eleventh Street NW, Second Floor
Washington, DC 20001

Association of Youth Museums
c/o Children's Museum of Memphis
1515 Central Avenue
Memphis, TN 38104

Canadian Museums Association
280 Metcalfe Street, Suite 400
Ottawa, ON K2P 1R7
Canada

Costume Society of America
55 Edgewater Drive
P.O. Box 73
Earleville, MD 21919

Council for Museum Anthropology
Southwest Museum
P.O. Box 41558
Los Angeles, CA 90041

Council of American Jewish Museums
c/o The Judaica Museums at the Hebrew Home for the Aged
    at Riverdale
5961 Palisade Avenue
Bronx, NY 10471

Council of American Maritime Museums
c/o South Street Seaport Museum
207 Front Street
New York, NY 10038

Independent Curators Incorporated
799 Broadway, Suite 205
New York, NY 10003

Internship Program, Office of Museum Programs
Smithsonian Institution
Arts & Industries Building, Room 2235
Washington, DC 20560

International Association of Museum Facility Administrators
P.O. Box 1505
Washington, DC 20013

International Council of Monuments and Sites
U.S. Committee (US/ICOMOS)
Decatur House
1600 H Street NW
Washington, DC 20006

International Museum Theatre Alliance
Museum of Science
Science Park
Boston, MA 02114

International Planetarium Society
c/o Hansen Planetarium
15 South State Street
Salt Lake City, UT 84111

Medical Museum Association
Museum of Medical History
1100 Euclid Avenue
Cleveland, OH 44106

Museum Computer Network
c/o Research and Scholar Office
National Museum of American Art
Smithsonian Institution
Washington, DC 20560

Museum Education Roundtable
P.O. Box 506
Beltsville, MD 20705

Museum Reference Center, Office of Museum Programs
A&I Building, Room 2235
Smithsonian Institution
Washington, DC 20560

Museum Store Association
One Cherry Center, Suite 460
Denver, CO 80222

Regional Museum Associations

New England Museums Association
Boston National Historical Park
Charleston Navy Yard
Boston, MA 02129

Mid-Atlantic Association of Museums
P.O. Box 817
Newark, DE 19715

Southeastern Museums Conference
P.O. Box 3494
Baton Rouge, LA 70821

Midwest Museums Conference
P.O. Box 11940
St. Louis, MO 63112

Mountain-Plains Museum Association
Box 335
Manitou Springs, CO 80829

Western Museums Conference
700 State Street, Room 130
Los Angeles, CA 90037

Botanical Specialists

American Association of Botanical Gardens and Arboreta
   (AABGA)
786 Church Road
Wayne, PA 19087

American Society of Consulting Arborists
5130 W 101st Circle
Westminster, CO 80030

International Society of Arboriculture
P.O. Box GG
Savoy, IL 61874

National Arbor Day Foundation/Institute
100 Arbor Avenue
Nebraska City, NE 68410

National Arborist Association
P.O. Box 1094
Amherst, NH 03031
Offers training programs for arborists.

Animal Behaviorists

American Association of Zoological Parks and Aquariums
American Zoo and Aquarium Association
7970-D Old Georgetown Road
Bethesda, MD 20114

Latham Foundation
Latham Plaza Building
Clement and Schillers Streets
Alameda, CA 94501

Dr. Mary Nitschke
Animal School, Inc.
Koll Business Center, Building 9
7850 SW Nimbus Avenue
Beaverton, OR 97005

About the Author

A full-time writer of career books, Blythe Camenson works hard to help job seekers make educated choices. She firmly believes that with enough information, readers can find long-term, satisfying careers. To that end, she researches traditional as well as unusual occupations, talking to a variety of professionals about what their jobs are really like. In all of her books she includes firsthand accounts from people who reveal what to expect in each occupation.

Camenson was educated in Boston, earning her B.A. in English and psychology from the University of Massachusetts and her M.Ed. in counseling from Northeastern University.

In addition to *Careers for Scholars & Other Deep Thinkers*, Camenson has written more than two dozen books for NTC/Contemporary Publishing Group, Inc.